Berliner ökophysiologische und phytomedizinische Schriften

Hrsg. von Christian Ulrichs und Carmen Büttner

Lebenswissenschaftliche Fakultät,
Humboldt-Universität zu Berlin

Band 40

Hrsg. von

Christian Ulrichs
Humboldt-Universität zu Berlin

und

Stefan Kühne
Julius-Kühn-Institut

Identification of variation within sex pheromone blends of various *Maruca vitrata* populations for refining pheromone lures and traps in Asia

DISSERTATION

zur Erlangung des akademischen Grades

Doctor rerum agriculturarum
(Dr. rer. agr.)
im Fach Agrarwissenschaften
eingereicht an der

Lebenswissenschaftlichen Fakultät der Humboldt-Universität zu Berlin

von
Diplom-Ingenieurin Stefanie Schläger
Geboren am 3.10.1984 in Hildesheim

Präsident der Humboldt-Universität zu Berlin
Prof. Dr. Jan-Hendrik Olbertz

Dekan der Lebenswissenschaftlichen Fakultät
der Humboldt-Universität zu Berlin
Prof. Dr. Richard Lucius

Gutachter

1. Prof. Dr. Dr. Christian Ulrichs
2. Prof. Dr. Stefan Kühne

Tag der mündlichen Prüfung: 21. Dezember 2015

Bibliografische Information der Deutschen Nationalbibliothek

Die Deutsche Nationalbibliothek verzeichnet diese Publikation in der
Deutschen Nationalbibliografie; detaillierte bibliografische Daten sind im Internet
über http://dnb.d-nb.de abrufbar.

1. Aufl. - Göttingen: Cuvillier, 2017

Zugl.: Berlin, Humboldt Universität, Diss., 2015

© CUVILLIER VERLAG, Göttingen 2017

Nonnenstieg 8, 37075 Göttingen

Telefon: 0551-54724-0

Telefax: 0551-54724-21

www.cuvillier.de

1. Auflage, 2017

Gedruckt auf umweltfreundlichem, säurefreiem Papier aus nachhaltiger Forstwirtschaft.

ISBN 978-3-7369-9570-3

eISBN 978-3-7369-8570-4

Table of Contents

1 Chapter I

General Introduction and Thesis Outline

1.1 The Legume Pod Borer as a Pest Insect

The legume pod borer, *Maruca vitrata* (Fabricius) (Lepidoptera: Crambidae) is a highly migratory species and is distributed throughout the tropics (Sharma et al. 1999; Kawazu et al. 2008). The host plants of *M. vitrata* belong mainly to the Fabaceae plant family (overview by Sharma et al. 1999), including several economically important legume crops. This insect species is a major pest of cowpea (*Vigna uniguiculata*) in sub-Saharan Africa (Sharma et al. 1999) and attacks yard long bean (*Vigna uniguiculata* spp. *sesquipedalis*) in Southeast Asia (Schreinemachers et al. 2014). *M. vitrata* causes severe economic losses in legumes, which are key dietary staples in many developing countries (Fery 2002). Because of the high protein content (Wills et al. 1984), they are considered as the "poor man's meat" (Winch 2007). Legumes are further used as cover crop against soil erosion (Hartwig and Ammon 2002) and as fodder crop for livestock (Sumberg 2002). Since legume plant roots are associated with nitrogen-fixing soil bacteria, plants also serve as green manure (Fujita and Ofosu-Budu 1996) to improve soil fertility (Giller 2001).

Adult *M. vitrata* moths (Fig. 1A) mate during the night (Jackai et al. 1990; Lu et al. 2007 and 2008) and females prefer to oviposit at the flower bud stage of the host plant (Sharma 1998). The eggs are laid singly or in clusters (Jackai et al. 1990; own observation, Fig 1B). An average of 400 eggs per female was recorded in laboratory bioassays revealing the high reproductive potential of this species (Jackai et al. 1990). *M. vitrata* develops through five larval stages (Fig. 1C) and a prepupal stage until pupation (Fig. 1D) (Adati et al. 2004). The shortest developmental period from hatching to pupation (12.2 ±SD 1.0 days) was observed at 29.3°C on a semi-synthetic diet in laboratory bioassays (Adati et al. 2004). Under these conditions, the pupal stage lasted 5.3 ±SD 0.6 days (females) and 5.9 ±SD 0.2 days (males). The larvae feed predominantly inside the reproductive plant organs, such as flowers, flower buds, and pods (Sharma et al. 1999). The larvae are not able to bore into the pods until the third larval stage (Sharma et al. 1999). Hence, the first-instar larvae prefer feeding on flowers, whereas the third- to fifth-instar larvae feed on the pods. In Nigeria, up to 80% of flowers were damaged in untreated cowpea fields (Afun et al. 1991).

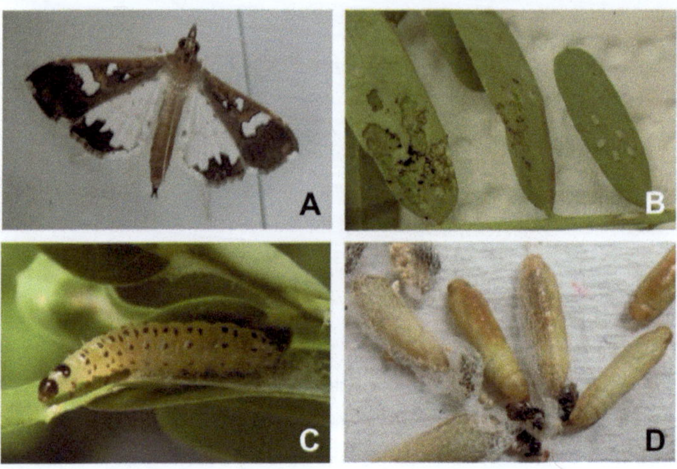

Figure 1 Developmental stages of *M. vitrata*: Male moth (A). Eggs and feeding damages of first-instar larvae on *Sesbania grandiflora* leaves (B). Fifth-instar larva on *S. grandiflora* leaves (C). Pupae (D).

The larvae are mainly controlled by synthetic insecticides (Srinivasan et al. 2013; Schreinemachers et al. 2014), but the results are not satisfactory because it is difficult to determine the most efficient time-point for pesticide application. Larval infestation of flowers shows hardly any external signs of damage (Sharma et al. 1999). Moreover, the larvae are protected from exogenous, adverse effects, e.g. natural enemies and insecticides, because of their internal feeding activity or webbing the inflorescences and leaves (Sharma et al. 1999). Furthermore, the development of pesticide resistances is a serious problem in pest control (Hajek 2004). Cases of insecticide resistance of *M. vitrata* have been reported more than a decade ago in Africa (Ekesi 1999) and in Southeast Asia (Ulrichs et al. 2001). Hence, there is an urgent need for an alternative and sustainable management strategy for *M. vitrata* in legume crops to minimize pesticide use. Successful integrated pest management strategies are often based on the combination of several components. Firstly, to prevent strong pest population growth, appropriate crop cultivation methods need to be established, such as planting of resistant or tolerant crop plants (Jackai et al. 1996; Bottenberg et al. 1998; Adekola and Oluleye 2008), optimal plant spacing (Asiwe et al. 2005), and intercropping (Karel 1993). Secondly, biopesticides and natural enemies can be used for direct control of *M. vitrata* eggs or larvae. Promising results have been reported for the usage of botanicals, such as crude aqueous extracts of black pepper, garlic bulb, and neem seed (Ekesi 2000), and microbial pesticides, such as nucleopolyhedrovirus (Lee et al. 2007), *Bacillus thuringiensis*

(Srinivasan 2008; Yule and Srinivasan 2013), as well as entomopathogenic fungi, for instance *Beauveria bassiana* and *Metarhizium anisopliae* (Ekesi et al. 2002; Mehinto et al. 2014; Tumehaise et al. 2015). Among invertebrates, the braconid wasp *Apanteles taragamae* showed the greatest potential as a biological control agent for *M. vitrata* in Taiwan (Huang et al. 2003), which has resulted in a series of studies to evaluate its introduction to Benin in West Africa (Dannon et al. 2010 a,b; 2012 a,b). Another important tool in integrated pest management is the use of pheromones for pest monitoring or mass trapping.

1.2 Lepidopteran Sex Pheromones and their Application in Pest Management

Pheromones are generally termed as "substances which are secreted to the outside by an individual and received by a second individual of the same species, in which they release a specific reaction" (Karlson and Lüscher 1959). Sex pheromones attract the conspecific opposite sex for mating (Jurenka 2004). Courtship of nocturnal Lepidoptera is mainly mediated by sex pheromones (Howse 1998) which are predominantly produced by females (Rafaeli and Jurenka 2003). In most cases, sex pheromone biosynthesis takes place in glands which are located between the 8th and 9th abdominal segment, as in the case of *Helicoverpa zea* (Raina et al. 2000) and is controlled by the pheromone biosynthesis activating neuropeptide (PBAN) produced in the brain-subesophageal ganglion complexes and released from the *corpora cardiaca* (Rafaeli 2005). For pheromone release, the female extrudes the pheromone gland from the abdomen, the so-called calling behavior (Groot 2014) which occurs for most moth species in the scotophase (Rafaeli and Jurenka 2003). The pheromone compounds are carried along by the wind forming an odor plume (Murlis et al. 1992). The conspecific male perceives the sex pheromones using specific receptors localized in hair-like sensilla on the antennae (Leal 2005) and locks onto the pheromone plume to locate the calling female for mating (Howse 1998). Most moth sex pheromones consist of a precise ratio of several compounds (Jurenka 2004) which are separated into three groups (Ando et al. 2004; Ando and Yamakawa 2011). The major group, Type I pheromones (75%), includes primary alcohols and their derivatives (mainly acetates and aldehydes) with a long straight chain (C10–C18). Type II pheromones (15%) are polyunsaturated hydrocarbons and their epoxy derivatives with a longer straight chain (C17–C23 and, exceptionally, C25 and C27). The remaining identified compounds are secondary alcohols and ketones with a straight chain and esters of a long unbranched-chain acid or methyl-branched compounds. Species specificity of pheromone blends is achieved by the structural diversity of pheromone compounds (polymorphic variation) and shifted pheromone ratios (monomorphic variation), whereas the latter is more common (Löfstedt 1990). Notably, pheromone blend variation does not only occur between species, but also between geographically different moth populations of the same species (McElfresh and Millar 1999; Gemeno et al. 2000; El-Sayed et al. 2003; Cortés et al. 2010).

Once the sex pheromone composition has been fully elucidated and synthesized, the pheromone blend can be applied on suitable dispensers and used as a species-specific lure in traps. Pheromone lures are mainly used for pest monitoring to determine the appropriate time for control measures (e.g. insecticide treatment) (Jones 1998). Pheromone lures can be also used for direct pest control as in mating disruption. This technique reduces or delays moth reproduction by saturating an area with synthetic pheromone, and thereby preventing odor-based communication and mate-finding (Jones 1998; Witzgall 2001). In pheromone-mediated mass trapping ("lure-and-kill technology"), high numbers of males are attracted and killed in the trap for example by insecticides (Jones 1998; Cork 2004).

For successful application of pheromone traps, the technical set up needs to be optimized for the target pest and adapted to the respective situation in the field. The presence of pheromone blend variation between populations of a pest species needs to be established, males may respond differently to synthetic pheromone lures in different regions, as for example observed in *Choristoneura rosaceana* Harris (Lepidoptera: Tortricidae) (El-Sayed et al. 2003). The chemical stability of the synthetic pheromones needs to be verified for field application as well as for storage conditions because it may have an impact on lure efficiency (Cork 2004). For example, aldehydes are known to react with atmospheric oxygen to form carboxylic acids (Stevens 1998). To prevent oxidation, synthetic pheromone lures are combined with antioxidants in a ratio of 1:1, for example with butylated hydroxytoluene (BHT) (Cork 2004). Pheromone components, which contain conjugated double bonds, are susceptible to photoisomerization induced by sunlight (Cork 2004). To prevent degradation of pheromone components by ultraviolet (UV) light, UV-stabilizers, such as 2-hydroxy-4-methoxybenzophenone (Ideses and Shani 1988), are loaded additionally on pheromone dispensers (Jones 1998).

Additionally, the pheromone dispenser needs to ensure a controlled release of the pheromone compounds in the field for the entire monitoring period (Cork 2004). The optimal trap design facilitates the entry and ensures the retention of the target pest (Cork 2004). Apart from the pest insect, the trap height depends on growth habit and cultivation method of the crop plant (Cork 2004).

1.3 Sex Pheromone Components and Blends of *M. vitrata*

The sex pheromone of *M. vitrata* has been investigated for more than a decade (Adati and Tatsuki 1999; Downham et al. 2003 and 2004). The first studies focused on insect populations from West Africa. (*E,E*)-10,12-hexadecadienal (*EE*10,12-16:Ald) was identified as the major pheromone component and (*E,E*)-10,12-hexadecadienol (*EE*10,12-16:OH) (Fig. 2) as a minor pheromone compound (at 3-4% of the aldehyde) in female gland extracts from Ghana by gas chromatography – electroantennographic detection (GC–EAD) and gas chromatography – mass spectrometry (GC–MS) (Adati and Tatsuki 1999). Both compounds were confirmed to be present in a mixed *M. vitrata* population from Benin, Nigeria, India, and Taiwan (Downham et al. 2003). Moreover, the authors presumed a monounsaturated hexadecenal in the pheromone blend based on GC–EAD results. Comparing a range of synthetic hexadecenal isomers by electroantennographic responses of *M. virata* males, (*E*)-10-hexadecenal (*E*10-16:Ald) (Fig. 2) elicited the highest response from the antennae. More recently, *E*10-16:Ald was directly detected in two Chinese *M. vitrata* populations (Huazhou and Wuhan) by GC–MS in addition to *EE*10,12-16:Ald, and *EE*10,12-16:OH (Lu et al. 2013). In fact, in females from Wuhan, the proportions of *E*10-16:Ald and *EE*10,12-16:Ald were comparable.

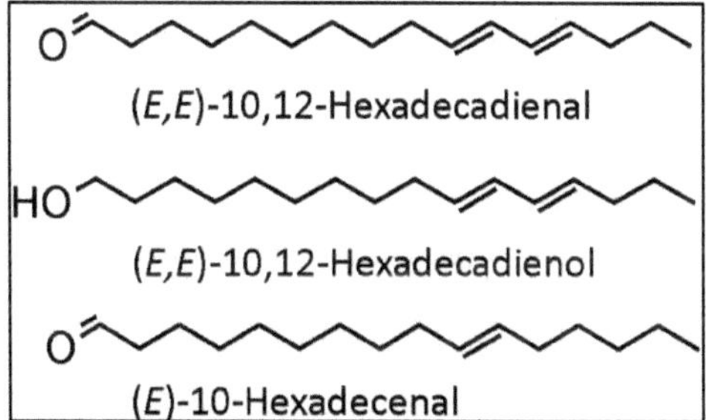

Figure 2 Structures of described *M. vitrata* pheromone components: (*E,E*)-10,12-Hexadecadienal, (*E,E*)-10,12-Hexadecadienol, and (*E*)-10-Hexadecenal.

In field studies, a pheromone ratio of 100:5:5 (*EE*10,12-16:Ald:*EE*10,12-16:OH:*E*10-16:Ald; 100:5:5-blend) was the most attractive blend in cowpea fields in Benin (Downham et al. 2003). Traps baited with this synthetic blend attracted more males than traps baited with two virgin females (Downham et al. 2003). In China, synthetic blends with a ratio of 100:10:80

and 100:10:10 attracted maximum numbers of males in field trapping experiments in Wuhan and Huazhou, respectively. However, *M. vitrata* trap catches by pheromone lures were generally very low. Only a total of 33.1 (±SE 2.4) males per trap were caught in Benin in eight weeks (Downham et al. 2003). In China, only 19.5 (±SD 3.6) and 17.8 (±SD 1.9) males in total per trap were trapped in Wuhan and Huazhou, respectively, in four weeks (Lu et al. 2013). In other regions of tropical Asia, *M. vitrata* males have never been caught by commercial pheromone lures so far (Srinivasan R. 2012, personal communication). In view of the fact that pheromone blend variation occurred between West African and Chinese *M. vitrata* populations (Downham et al. 2003; Lu et al. 2013), the failure of pheromone lures in tropical Asia might be linked to geographic variation as well.

Taken together, pheromone-mediated trapping of *M. vitrata* in the field is not successful to date. Hence, the aim of this thesis was to investigate pheromone blend composition and variation in *M. vitrata* to design efficient synthetic lures for field trapping.

Thesis Outline

In Chapter II, the focus is on the electrophysiological and behavioral responses of a Taiwanese *M. vitrata* population to the three described pheromone components, *EE*10,12-16:Ald, *EE*10,12-16:OH, and *E*10-16:Ald. In field trapping experiments in Taiwan, I tested the attractiveness of the 100:5:5-blend, which was the most efficient synthetic lure in Benin, and the major pheromone component *EE*10,12-16:Ald alone as synthetic lures. Moreover, female gland extracts and virgin females were used as attractants. Additionally, various trap designs and heights were evaluated in the field.

The pheromone blend composition of *M. vitrata* females from Taiwan and Thailand has not been identified so far. Therefore, Chapter III dealt with the analyses of the pheromone composition of the three described pheromone components in single female gland extracts from both regions by gas chromatography coupled with flame ionization detection. The detected pheromone ratios were then tested as synthetic attractants in field bioassays in Taiwan.

The three described pheromone components of *M. vitrata* are susceptible to chemical degradation, particularly under field conditions, which may lead to a loss of lure efficiency. *EE*-10,12-16:Ald and *EE*-10,12-16:OH contain conjugated double bonds, which are susceptible to photoisomerization induced by sunlight. Aldehydes, such as *EE*-10,12-16:Ald and *E*-10-16:Ald, may be oxidized by atmospheric oxygen. Therefore, the chemical stability of the pheromone components was investigated in Chapter IV. I conducted a stability test for the pheromone compounds, loaded together with butylated hydroxytoluene as antioxidant on rubber septa or polyethylene vials, under storage conditions for six weeks and simulated field conditions for one week. The remaining pheromone amounts were then quantified by GC–MS.

Possible geographic variation in the sexual communication between Asian and West African *M. vitrata* populations was the final objective of the thesis and experiments are presented in Chapter V. I conducted a comparative pheromone blend analysis of females from Taiwan, Thailand, Vietnam, and Benin using GC–MS. In wind tunnel experiments, the behavioral response of males from Taiwan and Benin to calling females and female gland extracts from both populations was assessed.

2. Chapter II

Developing Pheromone Lures for *Maruca vitrata* in Taiwan: Electrophysiological Responses of Males to Sex Pheromone Components and Field Evaluation of Pheromone Traps

Results communicated in <u>Schläger S, Ulrichs C, Srinivasan R, Beran F, Bhanu KRM, Mewis I and Schreiner M (2012) Developing pheromone traps and lures for *Maruca vitrata* in Taiwan. Gesunde Pflanzen 64 (4):183-186</u>

2.1 Abstract

Maruca vitrata is a pantropical pest on leguminous crops. In West Africa, a pheromone blend of three components, (E,E)-10,12-hexadecadienal, (E,E)-10,12-hexadecadienol, and (E)-10-hexadecenal, in a ratio 100:5:5 is used to monitor *M. vitrata* males in the field. In Asia, synthetic pheromone lures failed to attract this pest so far. Therefore, we studied a Taiwanese *M. vitrata* population to develop an efficient pheromone lure for this region. We analyzed the physiological response of *M. vitrata* antennae to the three described pheromone components by electroantennographic measurements. In subsequent field studies, we tested different synthetic pheromone lures, female gland extracts, and virgin females as attractants in Taiwan. In addition, we evaluated various trap designs and heights for trapping *M. vitrata*.

All previously described pheromone components elicited responses from Taiwanese *M. vitrata* male antennae. In dose-response tests, antennae were significantly more sensitive to (E,E)-10,12-hexadecadienal compared to (E,E)-10,12-hexadecadienol, and (E)-10-hexadecenal. However, neither synthetic lures nor dispensers baited with female gland extracts attracted males in field trapping experiments. In contrast, high numbers of males were caught in traps baited with live females. Plastic funnel traps caught no *M. vitrata*, but some moths were caught in delta traps. Trap height had no influence on trap catches in our studies.

2.2 Introduction

M. vitrata F. is a pantropical pest on economically important leguminous crops and is mainly controlled by insecticides (Srinivasan et al. 2013; Schreinemachers et al. 2014). However, control results are unsatisfying because larvae feed inside the plant organs and thus are protected from external effects (Sharma et al. 1999). Pheromone lures are used for pest monitoring and can help to perform target-oriented control measures.

Initial work on the sex pheromone of *M. vitrata* focused on West African insect populations where larvae cause severe damage on cowpea (*Vigna unguiculata*). (*E,E*)-10,12-hexadecadienal (*EE*10,12-16:Ald) and (*E,E*)-10,12-hexadecadienol (*EE*10,12-16:OH) were identified as pheromone components in gland extracts of *M. vitrata* females from Ghana (Adati and Tatsuki 1999) and a merged population from Taiwan, India, Benin and Nigeria (Downham et al. 2003) by gas chromatography – mass spectrometry (GC–MS) and gas chromatography – electroantennographic detection (GC–EAD). Downham et al. (2003) additionally suggested the presence of a monounsaturated hexadecenal in the pheromone blend of the mixed *M. vitrata* population based on GC–EAD results. Comparing a range of synthetic hexadecenal isomers by electroantennographic (EAG) responses, (*E*)-10-hexadecenal (*E*10-16:Ald) elicited the highest response from male antennae. A synthetic pheromone lure consisting of *EE*10,12-16:Ald, *EE*10,12-16:OH and *E*10-16:Ald in a ratio of 100:5:5 (100:5:5-blend) attracted significantly more males compared to other ratios in field trapping experiments in Benin (Downham et al. 2003).

M. vitrata is also a major pest on yard long beans (*Vigna unguiculata* spp. *sesquipedalis*) in Asia, particularly in Southeast Asia (Schreinemachers et al. 2014). However, commercially available pheromone lures so far did not attract any *M. vitrata* males in this region. Recently, Lu et al. (2013) found significant differences between pheromone blends of two different *M. vitrata* populations in China. To further study pheromone blend variability in this important pest species we investigated a Taiwanese *M. vitrata* population.

Here, we analyzed electrophysiological and behavioral responses of *M. vitrata* males from Taiwan towards the three pheromone components. Furthermore, we tested various trap designs and heights to optimize the application of pheromone traps against *M. vitrata*.

2.3 Methods and Materials

2.3.1 Dose-Response Test

Insects

M. vitrata F. larvae and pupae were obtained from AVRDC-The World Vegetable Center in Shanhua, Taiwan. At the Leibniz Institute of Vegetable and Ornamental Crops (IGZ) in Großbeeren, Germany, the larvae were reared in groups of 100 to 200 individuals in plastic containers (0.5 – 2 l) at least for one generation on artificial cowpea diet until pupation. The diet was prepared as described in Jackai and Raulston (1988) (Tab. 1), with three modifications. We added saccharose to the diet, but did not add dried and pulverized cowpea leaves, and used kanamycin (Sigma-Aldrich Chemie GmbH, Taufkirchen, Germany) as antibiotic. The pupae were transferred to acrylic glass or glass cages where the emerging moths mated. For oviposition, females were placed singly in small plastic cups (37 ml, Market Grounds GmbH & Co. KG). For experiments, pupae were placed separately in plastic cups (37 ml) and reared under a 14L:10D photoperiod at 25°C and 80% relative humidity in a controlled environment chamber (Vötsch). After emergence, moths were kept under the same conditions. Ten percent honey solution applied to dental rolls (Apodiscounter) was provided as food source.

Table 1 Composition of artificial diet for rearing *Maruca vitrata*.

Ingredients	Amounts in diet
H_2O (for blending)	800 ml
H_2O (for boiling agar)	1000 ml
Cowpea flour	225 g
Wheatgerm	63.6 g
Wesson salt mix	21.2 g
Ascorbic acid	12.5 g
Kanamycin	1 g
Agar	29.6 g
Saccharose	30 g
Methyl-parahydroxybenzoate	3.16 g
Sorbic acid	1.92 g
Potassium hydroxide (4M)	11 ml
Choline chloride (15%)	14.8 ml
Acetic acid (25%)	25 ml
Formaldehyde (10%)	13 ml
Vitamin powder	6 g

(Reference: Jackai and Raulston 1988)

Chemicals

Synthetic *EE*10,12-16:Ald (isomeric purity 99.6%), *EE*10,12-16:OH (>99.9%), and *E*10-16:Ald (>99.9%) were obtained from the Biocontrol Research Laboratories (BCRL) in Bangalore, India.

Electrophysiology

Electroantennographic experiments were performed at the Department of Evolutionary Neuroethology at the Max Planck Institute for Chemical Ecology (MPICE) in Jena, Germany. The antenna of a five-day-old male moth was cut at the base and 2 mm from the tip were removed. The distal and proximal ends of the antenna were each inserted into an Ag/AgCl glass capillary electrode filled with Ringer solution (Kaissling 1971). Antennal responses were amplified $10 \times$ by using a Universal AC/DC Probe connected to an IDAC 4 signal converter (Syntech). The three synthetic pheromone standards were diluted with hexane (Merck KGaA, $\geq$98.0%). Ten microliters of the diluted compounds (equivalent to a total final dose of 0.001, 0.01, 0.1, 1 and 10 µg) were applied as stimulus on filter paper disks (10×5 mm) in glass Pasteur pipettes. Pure hexane served as control. Odor pulses were puffed at 1-min intervals into a cleaned and humidified airstream. Airflow (0.8 l/min) and pulses (duration: 0.5 s) were controlled by a CS-55 stimulus controller (Syntech). Dose-response tests with concentration series of the three pheromone standards were performed with nine males. The absolute net EAG responses were calculated according to Lu et al. (2013). In brief, the mean absolute EAG responses of the control stimulations (hexane) preceding and following the test components were subtracted from the absolute EAG responses of the test components.

Statistical Analysis

Statistical analyses were conducted using SAS 9.4. Data was tested for normal distribution and homogeneity of variance. Depending on the outcome, data was analyzed using either one-way analysis of variance (ANOVA) followed by Tukey's range test or the non-parametric Kruskal-Wallis test with Bonferroni correction for pairwise multiple comparisons.

2.3.2 Lure and Trap Optimization Experiment

Synthetic Lures

Polyethylene vials (PE vials) baited with 1 mg of *EE*10,12-16:Ald or 1 mg of *EE*10,12-16:Ald, *EE*10,12-16:OH and *E*10-16:Ald in a ratio of 100:5:5 (100:5:5-blend) were used as pheromone dispensers (BCRL, India).

Field Tests

Unless otherwise noted, the field trapping experiments were conducted at the experimental site of AVRDC-The World Vegetable Center in Shanhua, Taiwan in June-July 2012 (weather station record; Tab. S2.1 and S2.2).

Experiment 1: The response of males to live females was tested by using delta traps baited with two virgin three-day-old female moths in yard long bean fields. Females were confined in a small plastic cup (37 ml; Fig. 1a), a tube made of wire (96 ml; Fig. 1b), or a big plastic cup (250 ml; Fig. 1c). All containers were sealed with mesh and fixed beneath the upper side of the delta trap. The trap design with females confined in a 250-ml-cup was tested in comparison with unbaited delta traps (control) for three nights with three replications in yard long bean fields.

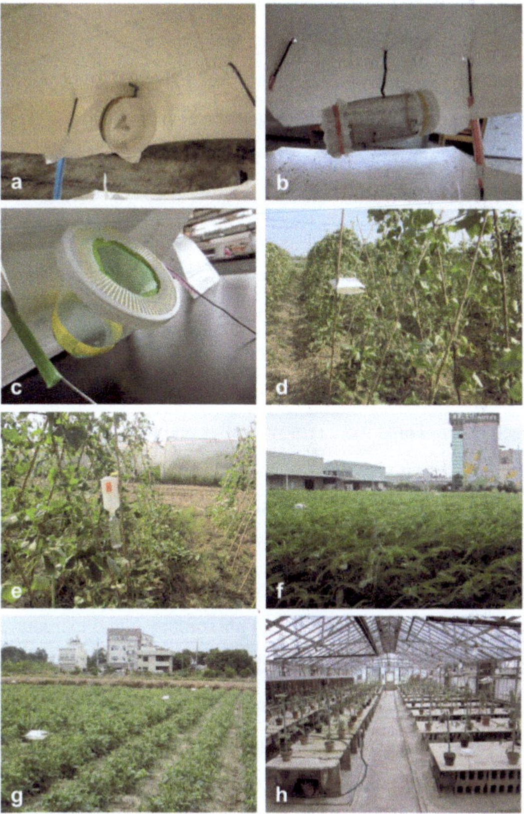

Figure 1 Trap designs and lures tested in field experiments in Taiwan. Delta trap baited with two *M. vitrata* females in a small plastic cup (37 ml) (a), in a tube made of wire (96 ml) (b), and in a big plastic cup (250 ml) (c). Delta trap in yard long bean field (d). Plastic funnel trap in yard long bean field (e). Delta traps in *Sesbania cannabina* field (f) and in mung bean field (g). Greenhouse cabin with potted mung bean plants and delta traps (h).

Experiment 2: Both synthetic lures were tested in sticky delta traps (Fig. 1d) and plastic funnel traps (Fig. 1e) with two windows (2 × 2 cm) on opposite sides in two heights (120 cm and 180 cm above ground) in a yard long bean field. Each lure was placed in the center of the trap using a small wire paper-clip; lures were replaced after two weeks and removed after another three weeks. Trap catches were counted weekly. The experiment was arranged in a randomized complete block design with three replications. The distance between traps was at least 20 m and the distance to the field edges was 5 m. Traps were set out after the flowering started and were suspended from bamboo sticks using wire.

Experiment 3: Delta traps baited with the synthetic pheromone lures were set up in a *Sesbania cannabina* field above the crop canopy (Fig. 1f). Unbaited delta traps served as control. Since the crop grew higher than the bamboo stick, the final trap height was about 2 m. Traps were arranged in a randomized complete block design with four replications. The distance between individual traps was 15 m and the distance to the field edges was at least 2 m. Trap catches were counted weekly over four weeks.

Experiment 4: Delta traps with the two synthetic lures and unbaited traps were additionally tested in five different *S. cannabina* fields in the district of Meinong in June 2012. Each field contained three traps (each synthetic lure and one unbaited control trap) and represented one replication. Traps were fixed at the level of crop height and the individual traps were placed 20 m apart from each other. Traps were removed after one week.

The same experimental design was used in the district of Kaohsiung in July 2012 in three different fields. The traps were removed after two weeks.

2.3.3 Lure Optimization Experiment - Gland Extracts as Lures

Field trapping experiments were conducted with pheromone gland extracts as lures in Taiwan. In this experiment, the attractiveness of gland extracts from different geographical regions was compared. Gland extracts and lures of females from Thailand, Malaysia and Benin were prepared at the IGZ in Germany and were shipped to Taiwan. Taiwanese gland extracts and lures were prepared at AVRDC – The World Vegetable Center.

Insects

M. vitrata pupae were shipped from the Malaysian Agricultural Research and Development Institute, Kuala Lumpur, Malaysia; the East and Southeast Asia Regional Office of AVRDC-The World Vegetable Center in Bangkok, Thailand, and the International Institute of Tropical Agriculture in Cotonou, Benin to the IGZ in Germany. Insects were reared as described in section 2.3.1.

In Taiwan, *M. vitrata* insects were collected from *S. cannabina* fields in the district of Meinong to establish an insect colony at AVRDC-The World Vegetable Center in Shanhua. Insects were reared under the natural circadian rhythm at 24-28°C and 70% relative humidity. The larvae were fed with *S. cannabina* leaves and the moths were supplied with honey and water.

Gland Extraction

At IGZ, pheromone glands were excised from four- to five-day-old virgin female moths five hours into scotophase and extracted in hexane (Merck KGaA, ≥98.0%) for 15 min (~20 glands in 200 µl). The supernatant was transferred into a new vial and was stored at -80°C until use.

At AVRDC-The World Vegetable Center, three- to four-day-old Taiwanese females showing calling behavior were dissected four to five hours after sunset. Gland extracts were prepared as described above and stored at -20°C.

Gas Chromatography – Mass Spectrometry (GC–MS)

The amount of the major pheromone component, *EE*10,12-16:Ald in gland extracts was quantified using GC–MS.

At IGZ, samples were analyzed using an Agilent 6890N GC equipped with an OPTIMA 5–MS fused silica capillary column (30 m x 0.25 mm ID, 0.25 µm film thickness, Macherey–Nagel, GmbH Co. KG) and a GERSTEL MultiPurpose Sampler coupled to an Agilent 5973 mass selective detector (MSD). Helium was used as carrier gas at a flow of 1 ml/min. One microliter of each sample was injected in splitless mode at 250°C. The oven program was 50°C for 3 min, increased with 10°C/min to 280°C and finally increased with 20°C/min to 300°C for 10 min to clean the column. Selected ion monitoring was used focusing on unique and the most abundant ions of *EE*10,12-16:Ald: m/z 67, 81, 95, 109, and 236. The retention time was determined by injecting the synthetic aldehyde. The amount of *EE*10,12-16:Ald in gland extracts was quantified by an external standard calibration curve (0.043, 0.427, 4.265, 42.65, 12.795, 21.325, 85.3, 106.625, 213.25, and 426.5 ng *EE*10,12-16:Ald).

In Taiwan, GC–MS analyses were performed at the National Cheng Kung University (NCKU) in Tainan using a SHIMADZU QP2010. The instrument was equipped with a J&W DB-5 column (30 m x 0.25 mm ID, 0.25 µm film thickness). Helium was used as carrier gas at a flow of 0.78 ml/min. Injections were performed in splitless mode at an injector temperature of 250°C. The oven program was 70°C held for 1 min and increased with 20°C/min to 300°C and hold for 5 min. MS was conducted using the scan mode (30–800 amu). For quantification, a calibration curve of synthetic *EE*10,12-16:Ald was prepared with the following concentrations: 4.26, 8.52, 42.6, 85.2 ng/µl.

Lure Preparation

Lures were prepared according to Cork (2004). Red rubber septa (10×20 mm, Wheaton) were washed three times with hexane and dried at room temperature in the fume hood. Septa were baited with gland extracts corresponding to 50 or 100 ng EE10,12-16:Ald. Therefore, the volume of the extract was adjusted to 100 µl with hexane (>98.0%, Merck) and then applied to the cup. The solvent was allowed to evaporate at room temperature and the rubber septa were stored in vials at -20°C until use. Rubber septa prepared at IGZ were sealed in crimp-capped vials and sent to AVRDC-The World Vegetable Center.

Field Test

Experiment 5: Gland extracts from virgin females from Benin and Taiwan (corresponding to 100 ng EE10,12-16:Ald) were used as lures in a yard long bean field in July 2012 using a randomized complete block design with three replications. Unbaited traps served as controls. Delta traps were placed at a height of 180 cm. Individual traps were positioned 20 m apart. Blocks were at least 50 m apart and were located in separate fields. The distance to the field edges was 5 m. Two replications were set out per treatment and block. Traps were removed after 2.5 weeks.

Experiment 6: Gland extracts from virgin females from Benin, Thailand, and Taiwan (corresponding to 50 ng EE10,12-16:Ald) were used as lures in a mung bean field (Fig. 1g) in July 2012. Delta traps were placed 20 cm above the crop canopy with two replications per treatment and one unbaited control trap. The distance between traps was 15 m and 4.5 m from the field edges. Since the natural infestation of plants was low, *M. vitrata* larvae (instars L3 to L5) were released on the mung bean plants two weeks prior to the experiment to increase the moth population during the trapping experiment. Additionally, several virgin two-day-old males were released in the mung bean field four days after traps were set out. Traps were removed after two weeks.

Greenhouse Experiment

Experiment 7: Potted mung bean plants were placed in a greenhouse cabin (Fig. 1h) with a maximum distance of 30-100 cm between individual plants (July 2012). Delta traps baited with gland extracts corresponding to 50 ng EE10,12-16:Ald of female moths from various *M. vitrata* populations (Benin, Malaysia, Taiwan, and Thailand) and an unbaited trap were placed 10 cm above the crop canopy. The distance between individual traps was 3 m. Six days after trap placement, 2 two- to three-day old virgin males were released in the greenhouse cabin. Traps were removed after two weeks.

Statistical Analysis

To compare trap catches of different treatments, the total number of moths caught per trap in the course of the experiment was log(x+1)-transformed and analysed by analysis of variance (ANOVA) using SAS 9.2©. Wilcoxon rank sum test was carried out for comparing trap catches of positive and negative control treatments.

2.4 Results

2.4.1 Dose-Response Test

Antennae of Taiwanese *M. vitrata* males responded to all three synthetic pheromone compounds (Fig. 2). *EE*10,12-16:Ald elicited the strongest response from male antennae. The EAG amplitude increased significantly at a dose of 0.1 µg. At doses between 0.1 – 10 µg, *EE*10,12-16:Ald elicited a significantly stronger response from male antennae compared to *EE*10,12-16:OH and *E*10-16:Ald. EAG responses between *EE*10,12-16:OH and *E*10-16:Ald did not differ significantly. However, the EAG response to *E*10-16:Ald increased significantly at a dose of 1 µg, whereas *EE*10,12-16:OH did not elicit a significant higher response from male antennae below a dose of 10 µg.

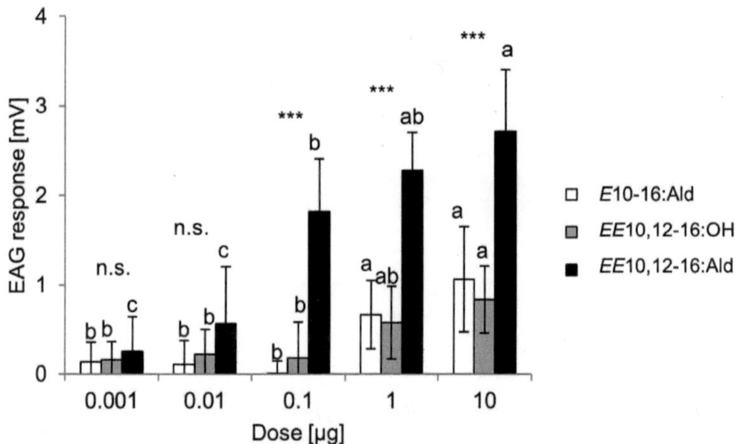

Figure 2 EAG responses (mean ±SD, N = 9) of Taiwanese *M. vitrata* male antennae to synthetic *EE*10,12-16:Ald, *EE*10,12-16:OH and *E*10-16:Ald. Different letters indicate significant differences between different doses of the same pheromone component (ANOVA with Tukey's range test or Kruskal-Wallis test followed by Bonferroni correction, $P \leq 0.05$). Significant differences above the histograms indicate that EAG responses differ significantly between *EE*10,12-16:Ald and both minor components, *EE*10,12-16:OH and *E*10-16:Ald (ANOVA with Tukey's range test or Kruskal-Wallis test followed by Bonferroni correction, $P \leq 0.05$; n.s. = no significant difference, *** ≤ 0.001).

<u>2.4.2 Field Tests</u>

In trapping experiments using *M. vitrata* females as positive control, only females confined in big plastic cups (250 ml) attracted males (Tab. 2) whereas traps baited with females confined in small plastic cups (37 ml) or tubes made of wire (96 ml) did not catch any *M. vitrata* males. However, trap catches varied strongly and depended on moth abundance and on conditions influencing flight activity. The highest number of males caught in a single trap during one night was 89 (Fig. 3).

Table 2 Trap catches of delta traps baited with 2 virgin females (3 days old, confined in 250-ml plastic cups) in yard long bean fields. Trap catch per night of *M. vitrata* males and females and non-target lepidopterans.

Lure	Non-target	Male	Female
2 females	0.33 ± 0.17 a	1.89 ± 0.51 a	0.11 ± 0.11 a
Blank	0.11 ± 0.11 a	0 b	0 a
Wilcoxon	0.298	< 0.001	0.374

Means (± SE) within a column followed by different letters indicate significant differences (N = 9; Wilcoxon rank sum test, $P \leq 0.05$).

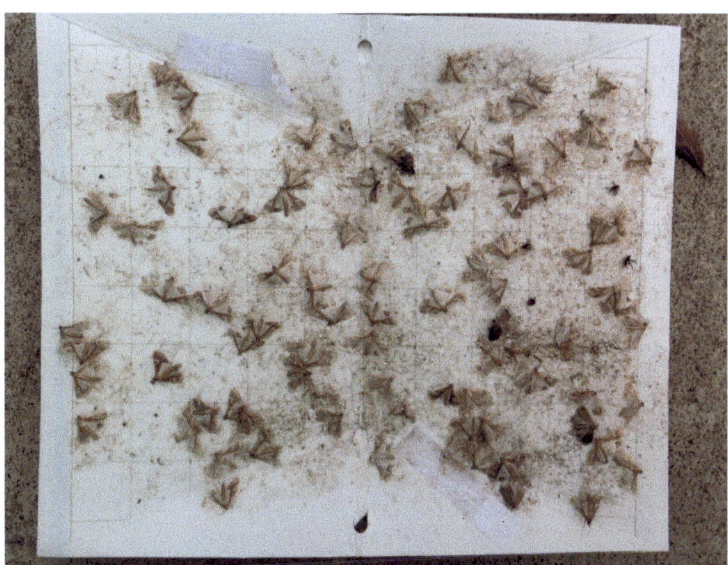

Figure 3 *Maruca vitrata* males caught in a delta trap baited with live females.

M. vitrata moths were only trapped in delta traps in the yard long bean field and trap height had no influence on trap catches (Tab. 3). In addition to *M. vitrata*, other lepidopterans, e.g.

Spodoptera litura, were also caught in the traps. However, delta traps baited with synthetic pheromone lures in the *S. cannabina* fields caught no *M. vitrata* moths. Moreover, traps baited with gland extracts from virgin *M. vitrata* females from different populations did not attract any *M. vitrata* males.

Table 3 Mean (± SE) of total catches/trap of *M. vitrata* in yard long bean fields using delta traps and lures containing 1 mg of *EE*10,12-16:Ald or of the 100:5:5-blend at two different trap heights.

Lure	Height [cm]	*M. vitrata*		
		Male	Female	Sex unknown
*EE*10,12-16:Ald	120	0 a	0.3 ± 0.3 a	0 a
	180	0 a	0 a	0.3 ± 0.3 a
100:5:5-blend	120	0 a	0.3 ± 0.3 a	0 a
	180	0.3 ± 0.3 a	0.3 ± 0.3 a	0.3 ± 0.3 a

Means within a column followed by the same letter were not significantly different ($N = 3$; $P \leq 0.05$, LSD following ANOVA).

2.5 Discussion

In these studies, we found that male antennae of *M. vitrata* from Taiwan responded to all three synthetic pheromone components. Although virgin female moths were highly attractive to *M. vitrata* males in field trapping experiments in Taiwan, males were not attracted to traps baited with synthetic pheromone compounds, or female gland extracts from various regions.

M. vitrata males from Taiwan were sensitive towards the three synthetic pheromone components. Lu et al. (2013) also detected a dose-response relationship towards the three components for *M. vitrata* populations from Wuhan and Huazhou by EAG measurements. In agreement with our results, *EE*10,12-16:Ald elicited the largest EAG response from antennae of males from both Chinese locations (Lu et al. 2013). EAG responses to *EE*10,12-16:OH and *E*10-16:Ald were low at a dose of 0.001 µg for the Huazhou population and at doses between 0.001 to 0.01 µg for the Wuhan population. However, the antennal response from Taiwanese males only increased significantly at a dose of 1 µg. These results indicate that Taiwanese males may be less sensitive towards *EE*10,12-16:OH and *E*10-16:Ald compared to males from both Chinese populations.

Delta traps baited with two virgin females confined in plastic cups (250 ml) were highly attractive in field trapping experiments in Taiwan. This result confirms that delta traps are appropriate for catching *M. vitrata* males. However, the cage size was crucial since females confined in a smaller plastic cup (37 ml) or a tube (96 ml) did not attract any males. Females may have disturbed each other in smaller cages which interfered with their calling behavior. This could be tested by baiting traps with only one female in cages differing in size. In contrast to our results, traps baited with two virgin females attracted significantly less *M. vitrata* males than traps baited with the 100:5:5-blend in field trapping experiments in Benin (Downham et al. 2003). The authors assumed that females were not constantly releasing pheromones compared to the synthetic lure. Based on our results, however, the cage size used to confine females in trapping experiments in Benin could also be responsible for the low attractiveness of live females.

The synthetic 100:5:5-blend did not attract *M. vitrata* males in field trapping experiments in Taiwan. Lures from the same batch did not attract males in Thailand and Vietnam either (Srinivasan et al. 2015). This blend was the most attractive lure in field studies in Benin and attracted a total of 33.1 (±2.4 SE) males per trap over eight weeks (Downham et al. 2003).

These findings indicate geographic variation in the sex pheromone blend between Asian and West African *M. vitrata* populations. Lu et al. (2013) recently found pheromone blend variation between two Chinese insect populations in field studies. A pheromone ratio of 100:10:80 (*EE*10,12-16:Ald: *EE*10,12-16:OH: *E*10-16:Ald) attracted the maximum number of males in Wuhan (total number of males caught per trap: 19.5 ±3.6 SD), whereas 100:10:10-blend was most attractive in Huazhou (17.8 ±1.9 SD).

It is possible that the amount of 1 mg of pheromone per dispenser might be too high for attracting *M. vitrata* males. Downham and co-workers loaded only 0.01 mg (2003) and 0.1 mg (2003, 2004) of the pheromone per dispenser which attracted *M. vitrata* males in Benin. In Wuhan and Huazhou, Lu et al. (2013) trapped the highest number of males when using 0.3 mg pheromone amount per lure. Notably, trap catches at a pheromone dose of 1 mg were not significantly different compared to the negative control in China (Lu et al. 2013).

Another possible explanation for the failure of pheromone lures is chemical instability of the pheromone compounds under field conditions. Aldehydes, such as *EE*10,12-16:Ald and *E*10-16:Ald, react with atmospheric oxygen to form carboxylic acids (Stevens 1998). To prevent oxidation, synthetic pheromone lures are combined with antioxidants, such as butylated hydroxytoluene (BHT), at a ratio of 1:1 (Cork 2004). Field studies with the cotton leaf-roller *Haritalodes derogata* (F.) (Lepidoptera: Crambidae) revealed that trap catches increased significantly by adding BHT to the pheromone lure comprising of *EZ*10,12-16:Ald and *EE*10,12-16:Ald (Himeno and Honda 1992). The missing antioxidant could explain why the 100:5:5-blend was not effective in field tests in Taiwan (Schläger et al. 2012), Thailand and Vietnam (Srinivasan et al. 2015). However, antioxidants were also not used in successful trapping experiments in China (Lu et al. 2013).

Furthermore, photoisomerization of synthetic pheromone lures may reduce their attractiveness. Conjugated diene systems, as present in *EE*10,12-16:Ald and *EE*10,12-16:OH, are susceptible to photoisomerization induced by sunlight (Cork 2004). Indeed, Adati and Tatsuki (1999) reported that *M. vitrata* males were more attracted to purified *EE*10,12-16:Ald (isomeric purity 99%) than to unpurified *EE*10,12-16:Ald (92%) in behavioral bioassays. Furthermore, the presence of stereoisomers reduced male attraction, especially when adding *EZ*10,12-16:Ald to *EE*10,12-16:Ald (Adati and Tatsuki 1999). Also in field bioassays with *Earias vittella* F. (Lepidoptera: Noctuidae), the addition of an isomer (*EZ*10,12-16:Ald) to the major pheromone component *EE*10,12:16Ald significantly reduced trap catches (Cork et al. 1988). Synthetic lures for field studies in Benin (Downham et al 2003), China (Lu et al. 2013), Taiwan (Schläger et al. 2012), Thailand, and Vietnam (Srinivasan et al. 2015) were not merged with UV-stabilizers to prevent photoisomerization. Conversely, trap catches of *M. vitrata* males in field studies in Benin were not affected by different isomeric purities of *EE*10,12-16:Ald and *EE*10,12-16:OH (73%, 80%, 91%, or >99%) (Downham et al. 2004). Additionally, pheromone lures for field trapping experiments in Benin were wrapped in aluminum foil to prevent photoisomerization (Downham et al. 2003, 2004), but there was again no difference between male trap catches with protected or exposed pheromone dispensers (Downham et al. 2004).

The infestation of the crops by *M. vitrata* strongly decreased end of June 2012 according to heavy rain falls and flooded fields (Tab. S2.1). The low *M. vitrata* population might also explain why gland extracts as lures did not attract any males in the field. Since *M. vitrata* infestation in the field is highest April to May, the response to gland extracts in comparison to live females should be tested again in the appropriate season.

Funnel traps could not be evaluated as trap design, since the synthetic lures were not attractive for Taiwanese *M. vitrata* males. Moreover, the funnel trap did not provide enough space for females as lures to test this trap design as a positive control. Downham et al. (2004) trapped significantly more males in a plastic funnel trap (22 cm high × 15 cm outside diameter; Agrisense-BCS, Pontypridd, UK) or in plastic jerry cans (2 and 5 liter, vegetable oil containers), with four windows (at least 4 × 6.5 cm) one on each side, than in delta traps. The authors pointed out that funnel traps and plastic cans were omni-directional compared to the bi-directional delta traps. Hence, there may be a higher chance of males encountering the pheromone plume during cross-wind orientation flights from omni-directional traps. The influence of the trap height could not be evaluated using the synthetic lures. However, we did not test delta traps baited with females at different trap heights, due to time constraints.

In conclusion, synthetic pheromone lures are not available to monitor the Taiwanese *M. vitrata* population. We have shown that Taiwanese males are sensitive towards the three described pheromone components. It might be possible that Taiwanese females produce a divergent pheromone ratio. Therefore, the pheromone composition of this *M. vitrata* population should be investigated by chemical analysis. For future field studies, the chemical stability of the pheromone components must be addressed. Pheromone lures should be prepared with antioxidants and UV-stabilizers.

2.6 Supplementary Material

Table S2.1 AVRDC-The World Vegetable Center: Weather Station Record June 2012

| DATE | Atmospheric Pressure [hPa] | | Humidity [%] | | | Air Temperature °C | | | Soil Temperature °C | | | | | | Wind | | Solar Intensity | Preci-pitation | Eva-poration |
| | | | | | | | | | 10 cm | | | 30 cm | | | Speed | Dir | | | |
	Max	Min	Max	Min	Mean	Max	Min	Mean	Max	Min	Mean	Max	Min	Mean	m/s	deg	w-h/m2	mm	mm
01.06.2012	1007.0	1003.0	91.5	49.0	73.7	34.0	23.8	28.1	30.3	27.9	29.0	29.1	28.4	28.8	1.5	267.9	6571.6	0.0	7.2020
02.06.2012	1006.0	1001.0	97.3	44.1	77.4	34.3	23.8	28.0	30.5	28.1	29.2	29.3	28.6	28.9	2.2	237.6	7793.3	0.0	9.0270
03.06.2012	1003.0	999.0	94.9	42.8	76.2	36.1	23.6	28.2	30.4	28.0	29.1	29.3	28.7	29.0	1.8	188.4	6486.9	0.0	6.5310
04.06.2012	1002.0	999.0	95.2	50.1	78.9	34.3	24.4	28.2	30.1	28.3	29.1	29.3	28.8	29.1	1.9	149.9	5512.9	0.0	5.1520
05.06.2012	1004.0	1001.0	98.0	49.3	80.4	34.3	24.4	28.2	30.5	28.2	29.3	29.4	28.7	29.1	1.9	231.1	7005.8	0.0	6.5660
06.06.2012	1005.0	1002.0	97.3	47.5	75.3	34.6	24.3	29.0	30.6	28.4	29.4	29.6	28.9	29.2	1.2	265.6	6508.6	0.0	5.5320
07.06.2012	1006.0	1002.0	93.6	47.2	71.0	36.2	26.3	30.5	30.3	28.8	29.6	29.7	29.2	29.4	1.8	157.1	6822.1	0.0	7.7890
08.06.2012	1006.0	1004.0	97.2	49.8	82.7	35.1	26.0	29.0	29.8	28.5	29.1	29.6	29.1	29.3	1.9	163.6	4901.7	14.2	0.9430
09.06.2012	1006.0	1002.0	100.0	66.8	92.5	32.9	24.9	27.2	29.0	26.8	28.3	29.3	28.3	28.9	2.0	148.4	3499.5	91.0	0.0170
10.06.2012	1003.0	999.0	99.9	73.7	91.3	31.2	24.7	27.2	28.6	26.3	27.2	28.4	27.3	27.8	2.5	171.3	2830.5	95.0	3.0110
11.06.2012	1001.0	997.0	99.7	74.9	87.8	31.0	25.8	28.5	28.3	27.2	27.8	28.1	27.7	27.9	3.2	221.0	2533.0	30.4	1.2470
12.06.2012	1000.0	996.0	99.9	83.4	95.5	29.0	24.9	26.8	28.0	27.1	27.5	28.0	27.6	27.8	2.6	221.5	640.1	67.4	0.7490
13.06.2012	1002.0	998.0	99.9	62.9	90.4	33.5	24.7	27.4	28.5	27.0	27.6	27.9	27.3	27.6	1.3	143.4	3247.1	5.4	0.1110
14.06.2012	1002.0	997.0	100.0	88.9	97.6	27.2	23.6	25.1	27.5	25.9	26.6	27.9	26.9	27.4	2.3	144.9	601.5	204.6	0.8910
15.06.2012	1002.0	998.0	97.9	70.0	91.1	31.4	25.2	26.8	27.5	26.0	26.6	27.1	26.6	26.8	2.6	162.3	3527.9	8.0	0.1130
16.06.2012	1004.0	1000.0	97.4	47.0	80.2	35.1	24.9	28.4	28.0	26.3	27.0	27.5	26.8	27.1	2.0	175.6	5025.1	0.2	3.4270
17.06.2012	1005.0	1002.0	100.0	48.9	84.4	34.2	24.3	28.1	29.1	27.0	27.9	28.0	27.4	27.5	1.5	169.5	5322.8	59.6	3.9340
18.06.2012	1004.0	999.0	100.0	48.5	78.6	35.0	24.4	28.9	28.6	27.0	27.8	28.0	27.4	27.7	1.8	153.9	6681.8	4.8	4.2260
19.06.2012	1001.0	997.0	99.7	82.0	95.6	29.7	24.9	26.1	28.3	27.0	27.6	28.0	27.6	27.8	2.4	150.2	2155.4	86.2	3.6120
20.06.2012	1002.0	994.0	99.9	87.4	95.3	27.0	23.3	25.4	27.3	25.7	26.5	27.7	26.8	27.2	4.3	189.3	320.1	132.8	3.2560
21.06.2012	1006.0	1001.0	100.0	88.9	96.3	27.5	22.9	25.2	26.7	25.4	26.0	26.9	26.3	26.5	1.5	154.0	1563.4	31.4	0.1990
22.06.2012	1007.0	1004.0	98.9	71.6	90.5	31.2	24.4	27.0	27.1	25.7	26.3	26.8	26.3	26.5	2.0	162.3	3258.4	6.6	1.1940
23.06.2012	1007.0	1004.0	96.6	59.9	88.8	32.8	25.1	27.2	27.4	26.0	26.6	27.0	26.6	26.8	2.1	155.8	3646.3	14.4	0.8250
24.06.2012	1007.0	1005.0	96.9	45.1	76.7	34.2	24.7	28.8	27.9	26.1	27.0	27.4	26.8	27.0	2.2	169.8	6065.0	3.8	3.2670
25.06.2012	1006.0	1004.0	96.6	48.2	76.1	34.1	24.7	29.2	28.6	26.6	27.5	27.8	27.2	27.4	2.0	177.9	6109.8	0.0	6.8430
26.06.2012	1007.0	1004.0	99.1	49.5	77.1	34.3	24.5	29.1	28.9	27.1	27.9	28.1	27.6	27.8	1.9	179.2	6212.7	0.0	6.6180
27.06.2012	1007.0	1005.0	98.5	40.9	75.0	35.9	23.9	29.4	29.6	27.1	28.3	28.6	27.8	28.1	1.4	177.0	7073.7	0.0	7.3030
28.06.2012	1007.0	1000.0	96.8	47.8	78.8	34.4	25.5	29.1	29.8	28.0	28.8	28.9	28.4	28.6	1.9	184.2	6241.7	0.0	7.0910
29.06.2012	1006.0	999.0	95.0	55.8	79.1	33.9	26.3	28.8	29.6	28.1	28.7	28.9	28.6	28.8	1.5	190.2	3520.0	0.6	3.4890
30.06.2012	1010.0	1005.0	97.2	40.6	71.4	37.0	24.7	30.3	29.9	27.6	28.7	29.0	28.4	28.6	1.2	98.4	6417.9	0.2	5.9460
TOTAL	30141.0	30021.0	2934.9	1762.4	2505.6	991.2	738.7	839.1	866.4	813.1	838.0	850.5	831.9	840.3	60.3		138096.5	856.6	116.1110
MEAN	1004.7	1000.7	97.8	58.7	83.5	33.0	24.6	28.0	28.9	27.1	27.9	28.3	27.7	28.0	2.0		4603.2	28.6	3.8704

Table S2.2 AVRDC-The World Vegetable Center: Weather Station Record July 2012

DATE	Atmospheric Pressure [hPa]		Humidity [%]			Air Temperature °C			Soil Temperature °C						Wind		Solar Intensity	Preci-pitation	Eva-poration
										10 cm			30 cm		Speed	Dir			
	Max	Min	Max	Min	Mean	Max	Min	Mean	Max	Min	Mean	Max	Min	Mean	m/s	deg	w-h/m2	mm	mm
01.07.2012	1011.0	1007.0	98.7	41.8	72.1	35.7	25.0	30.2	30.5	28.1	29.2	29.3	28.7	29.0	1.3	213.4	6877.3	0.0	7.3360
02.07.2012	1011.0	1006.0	98.3	49.7	78.8	34.5	24.8	29.4	30.4	28.4	29.4	29.5	29.0	29.2	1.4	201.4	6111.9	1.2	5.5870
03.07.2012	1007.0	1003.0	98.8	42.6	75.3	35.5	25.2	29.7	31.1	28.5	29.7	29.8	29.1	29.4	1.2	212.7	6545.9	0.0	4.5640
04.07.2012	1007.0	1003.0	91.6	46.6	73.6	36.0	26.5	29.9	31.4	28.8	30.0	30.0	29.3	29.6	1.8	184.3	6324.3	0.0	7.3720
05.07.2012	1009.0	1005.0	96.4	43.0	77.7	36.7	25.8	29.7	31.2	28.7	30.0	30.1	29.4	29.8	1.4	206.5	5555.9	0.0	6.2330
06.07.2012	1009.0	1006.0	96.9	46.6	79.4	35.7	25.7	29.1	30.6	28.7	29.5	30.0	29.5	29.7	1.7	149.6	4391.1	0.6	4.6480
07.07.2012	1008.0	1005.0	99.0	42.6	72.6	35.0	24.4	29.7	30.6	27.9	29.2	29.7	29.0	29.3	1.6	181.5	6820.1	0.0	7.6730
08.07.2012	1008.0	1004.0	97.9	46.2	75.5	34.9	25.1	29.7	30.9	28.3	29.6	29.9	29.2	29.5	1.3	176.7	6046.2	0.0	6.7460
09.07.2012	1008.0	1006.0	95.5	38.5	71.5	35.6	25.0	29.8	32.0	28.4	30.1	30.3	29.3	29.7	1.3	215.4	7919.2	0.0	8.4430
10.07.2012	1008.0	1005.0	92.7	38.5	71.3	35.0	25.2	29.9	32.0	28.6	30.2	30.4	29.6	29.9	1.6	213.7	7585.3	0.0	7.4800
11.07.2012	1007.0	1005.0	95.9	42.1	72.7	34.4	26.1	29.9	31.9	28.9	30.3	30.4	29.7	30.1	1.8	199.2	7194.3	0.0	7.6190
12.07.2012	1008.0	1006.0	94.4	38.6	69.8	35.1	25.3	29.8	33.4	28.5	30.7	31.0	29.7	30.2	1.8	204.0	7938.9	0.0	7.7010
13.07.2012	1008.0	1005.0	94.8	35.2	69.7	35.5	25.2	29.7	32.6	28.8	30.6	30.9	30.0	30.4	1.7	188.9	6178.5	0.0	6.8540
14.07.2012	1007.0	1004.0	91.8	34.6	71.8	35.4	26.1	29.8	32.2	29.0	30.5	30.8	30.0	30.4	2.2	166.9	5931.5	0.2	6.0400
15.07.2012	1007.0	1005.0	95.3	48.3	76.0	34.4	25.9	29.2	32.0	29.0	30.4	30.7	29.9	30.3	1.9	148.0	5590.4	1.8	4.0850
16.07.2012	1008.0	1006.0	91.6	47.2	73.6	34.6	25.8	29.6	31.9	28.8	30.2	30.6	29.8	30.2	1.8	168.0	4810.8	0.0	4.1190
17.07.2012	1008.0	1005.0	94.7	41.0	70.9	35.0	24.9	29.9	33.9	28.5	30.9	31.2	29.7	30.3	1.6	187.0	7558.9	0.0	9.2020
18.07.2012	1007.0	1005.0	94.3	53.2	80.8	33.5	25.5	28.1	31.2	29.0	30.1	31.1	30.1	30.4	1.0	135.9	3137.4	2.0	1.3140
19.07.2012	1007.0	1004.0	99.0	41.0	77.4	35.3	24.5	29.0	34.2	28.2	30.6	31.0	29.4	30.1	1.2	177.5	7208.1	4.6	5.4080
20.07.2012	1006.0	1001.0	99.0	53.6	81.1	33.6	25.3	29.2	32.4	28.7	30.4	30.7	29.7	30.2	1.2	197.1	4789.1	0.0	3.3070
21.07.2012	1003.0	1000.0	97.0	43.6	79.7	36.3	25.1	29.4	33.1	29.2	30.7	31.1	30.0	30.5	1.7	148.7	5886.2	15.0	4.8300
22.07.2012	1002.0	999.0	98.6	50.3	88.4	34.7	25.0	27.3	31.6	28.3	29.3	30.7	29.5	30.0	1.3	113.1	3567.3	41.2	0.1040
23.07.2012	1003.0	999.0	97.2	45.4	79.2	35.6	25.0	28.9	32.3	28.0	29.8	30.3	29.1	29.6	1.5	162.4	5465.2	0.2	4.1240
24.07.2012	1007.0	1002.0	99.5	49.6	85.4	34.7	23.4	27.7	31.7	27.4	29.4	30.3	29.1	29.8	1.5	161.8	3706.4	39.2	2.3850
25.07.2012	1008.0	1005.0	99.8	56.2	89.8	32.6	23.6	26.1	30.1	26.2	27.8	29.2	28.0	28.7	1.2	119.0	3131.0	61.2	1.9130
26.07.2012	1007.0	1004.0	99.7	54.6	80.1	33.0	23.9	27.7	31.0	26.4	28.3	29.2	27.7	28.2	1.2	215.4	6039.1	0.4	4.1710
27.07.2012	1005.0	1003.0	95.9	52.7	77.5	33.6	24.6	28.3	31.2	27.8	29.4	29.7	28.7	29.1	1.1	175.7	4774.8	0.0	5.2530
28.07.2012	1005.0	1003.0	95.5	50.6	78.6	33.6	23.8	27.6	30.8	27.7	29.1	29.7	28.8	29.2	0.8	167.2	4258.3	0.0	3.7000
29.07.2012	1004.0	999.0	98.5	47.7	78.4	35.7	24.8	29.2	32.1	28.2	30.1	30.3	29.0	29.5	1.4	202.7	6095.9	0.0	6.4070
30.07.2012	1000.0	994.0	94.3	55.9	77.2	32.5	25.7	29.3	31.2	28.8	30.1	30.3	29.5	29.9	1.4	171.3	4046.9	0.0	4.3240
31.07.2012	995.0	988.0	96.9	68.5	89.4	30.7	25.7	27.8	30.3	28.8	29.6	30.2	29.5	29.8	1.3	141.2	2108.5	3.4	0.1880
TOTAL	31198.0	31092.0	2989.5	1445.9	2395.3	1074.2	777.6	900.3	981.7	878.7	925.1	938.2	908.7	922.3	45.4		173594.6	171.0	159.1300
MEAN	1006.4	1003.0	96.4	46.6	77.3	34.7	25.1	29.0	31.7	28.3	29.8	30.3	29.3	29.8	1.5		5599.8	5.5	5.1332

3 Chapter III

Pheromone Blend Analysis of *Maruca vitrata* Populations from Tropical Asia and Field Evaluation of Synthetic Pheromone Blends in Taiwan

Results communicated at

- 48. Gartenbauwissenschaftliche Jahrestagung 2013, Rheinische Friedrich-Wilhelms-Universität Bonn. (Schläger S, Ulrichs C, Beran F, Schreiner M und Mewis I. (2013) Optimierung der Fängigkeit von *Maruca vitrata* durch Pheromonfallen. BHGL – Schriftenreihe Band 29, 2013, p. 28)

- International Chemical Ecology Conference, Melbourne Convention & Exhibition Centre (Schläger S, Ulrichs C, Beran F, Groot AT, Srinivasan R, Lin M-Y, Yule S, Bhanu KRM, Schreiner M and Mewis I (2013) Pheromone blend variation of *Maruca vitrata* and investigations on pheromone stability for refining lures in Southeast Asia. Book of abstracts p.178)

3.1 Abstract

The legume pod borer, *Maruca vitrata*, is a pantropical pest on leguminous crops. A pheromone lure comprised of (E,E)-10,12-hexadecadienal, (E,E)-10,12-hexadecadienol, and (E)-10-hexadecenal in a ratio of 100:5:5 attracted moths in field trapping experiments in Benin. However, this blend was not attractive in field trapping experiments in Taiwan, Thailand, and Vietnam. In order to develop efficient synthetic pheromone lures for monitoring *M. vitrata* in Asia, we investigated the pheromone composition of *M. vitrata* females from Taiwan and Thailand. In subsequent field bioassays, we tested the newly detected pheromone blends as attractants in Taiwan.

The presence of the previously described pheromone components was confirmed in both Asian *M. vitrata* populations by gas chromatography – flame ionization detection, but the ratios differed from the one attracting male *M. vitrata* in Benin. (E,E)-10,12-hexadecadienol accounted for about 50% of the pheromone blend in both Asian populations. We found that (E,E)-10,12-hexadecadienol in particular was unstable in pheromone gland extracts and was detectable only in traces after one week. In field trapping experiments in Taiwan, the attractiveness of the determined pheromone blends (Taiwan- and Thailand-blend) was analyzed. However, the corresponding synthetic lures did not attract *M. vitrata* males in Taiwan.

3.2 Introduction

Maruca vitrata is a pantropical pest of economically important leguminous crops and is controlled mainly by synthetic insecticides (Srinivasan et al. 2013; Schreinemachers et al. 2014). However, pest control is not satisfying because the larvae are exposed on the host plant only for a short time after hatching (Srinivasan et al. 2013). Most of the time, larvae feed inside of the plant organs and are not efficiently affected by pesticides (Sharma et al. 1999). Pest monitoring by pheromone traps can help to perform target-oriented control measures.

The first pheromone analysis of *M. vitrata* was performed using females from Ghana (Adati and Tatsuki 1999). The authors identified (*E,E*)-10,12-hexadecadienal (*EE*10,12-16:Ald) as the major pheromone component by gas chromatography – electroantennographic detection (GC–EAD) and gas chromatography – mass spectrometry (GC–MS). The corresponding alcohol (*E,E*)-10,12-hexadecadienol (*EE*10,12-16:OH) was also detected by GC–MS but only at 3–4% compared to the aldehyde. However, the addition of *EE*10,12-16:OH to *EE*10,12-16:Ald did not increase male response in behavioral bioassays (Adati and Tatsuki 1999). Downham and coworkers (2003) confirmed both components in a mixed *M. vitrata* population from Benin, Nigeria, India, and Taiwan. In addition to these two compounds, the authors assumed a monounsaturated hexadecenal based on GC–EAD experiments. In electroantennographic (EAG) measurements, (*E*)-10-hexadecenal (*E*10-16:Ald) elicited the largest response from male antennae among a range of synthetic hexadecenal isomers. A synthetic pheromone lure consisting of *EE*10,12-16:Ald, *EE*10,12-16:OH and *E*10-16:Ald in a ratio of 100:5:5 (100:5:5-blend) attracted significantly more *M. vitrata* males compared to other pheromone ratios in field trapping experiments in Benin (Downham et al. 2003). However, this blend did not attract males in Taiwan (Schläger et al. 2012), Thailand, and Vietnam (Srinivasan et al. 2015). These variable trapping results may be explained by geographic variation of the pheromone composition between Asian and West African *M. vitrata* populations. A comparative study of two geographically different Chinese *M. vitrata* populations indeed recently revealed geographic variation in pheromone blends and sexual attraction to synthetic lures (Lu et al. 2013). Females from Huazhou produced a pheromone ratio of 100:0.7:10.3 (*EE*10,12-16:Ald:*EE*10,12-16:OH:*E*10-16:Ald), whereas the pheromone ratio of females from Wuhan comprised a high proportion of *E*10-16:Ald: 100:12.1:79.5. The different pheromone blends were confirmed in subsequent field studies. A 100:10:10-blend attracted the highest number of males from Huazhou (total number of males caught per trap: 17.8 ±1.9 SD), whereas males from Wuhan were mainly attracted by the 100:10:80-blend (19.5 ±3.6 SD).

Since *M. vitrata* is also a major pest of economically important yard long bean (*Vigna unguiculata* spp. *sesquipedalis*) in tropical Asia, e.g. in Thailand and Vietnam (Schreinemachers et al. 2014), the development of pheromone traps for this region is urgently needed. In our studies, we investigated the pheromone composition of *M. vitrata* populations from Thailand and Taiwan. Single gland extracts were analyzed by gas chromatography coupled with flame ionization detection (GC–FID) following the method of Dr. Astrid T. Groot from the Department of Entomology at the Max Planck Institute for Chemical Ecology (MPICE), Jena, Germany. The discovered pheromone ratios were tested as attractants in subsequent field trapping experiments in Taiwan.

3.3 Methods and Materials

3.3.1 Pheromone Gland Extraction

Insects

M. vitrata pupae were obtained from AVRDC – The World Vegetable Center in Shanhua, Taiwan, and in Bangkok, Thailand. The insects were reared at the Leibniz-Institute of Vegetable and Ornamental Crops, Großbeeren/Erfurt e.V. (IGZ), Germany, as described in section 2.3.1. For experiments, female pupae were kept singly in small plastic cups (37 ml, Market Grounds GmbH & Co.KG) at 25°C and 80% relative humidity under a 14L:10D photoperiod in a controlled environment chamber (Vötsch). After emergence, moths were supplied with 10% honey solution.

Pheromone Gland Extraction

Ovipositors containing the pheromone gland were excised from four- to five-day-old virgin female moths four to five hours into scotophase. Glands were placed singly in 150 µl conical glass inserts (Macherey-Nagel) containing 50 µl hexane and 50 ng pentadecane ($\geq$99.8%, Sigma-Aldrich) as internal standard. Glands were extracted for 30–40 min at room temperature in 1.5 ml brown glass vials (Macherey-Nagel) to prevent photoisomerization of conjugated diene systems (Ideses and Shani 1988; Cork 1988 and 2004). After incubation, gland tissue was removed and gland extracts were stored at -80°C for up to 11 days until analysis.

Chemicals

Synthetic *EE*10,12-16:Ald (isomeric purity 97.5%), *EE*10,12-16:OH (92.2%), and *E*10-16:Ald (>99.9%) were obtained from Biocontrol Research Laboratories (BCRL) in Bangalore, India.

Gas Chromatography – Flame Ionization Detection

At the MPICE (Department of Entomology), Jena, gland extracts were reduced under a gentle stream of N_2 to 1–2 µl, taken up into 1-2 µl octane, and placed in a 150 µl conical glass insert (Macherey-Nagel) within a crimp-capped vial. Samples were analyzed using an HP7890 gas chromatograph (GC) equipped with a DB-WAXetr column (30 m × 0.25 mm × 0.5 µm, Agilent) coupled to a flame ionization detector (FID). The entire volume was injected in splitless mode using an automatic injector (7683, Agilent). The inlet temperature was 250°C. The oven program was 60°C held for 2 min, increased with 30°C/min to 180°C, then with

5°C/min to 230°C to separate the pheromone compounds, and finally heated at 20°C/min to 245°C held for 15 min to clean the column before the next analysis. The carrier gas was helium at a flow of 1.514 ml/min. A multicomponent blend containing the three synthetic pheromone components was injected under the same conditions and retention times were compared with compounds present in the gland extracts.

Statistical Analysis

The relative amounts of each pheromone component between the populations were compared by a multivariate analysis of variance (MANOVA) using SAS 9.4. The means were separated using least-square means (LSMEANS) with Tukey's range test for multiple comparisons.

3.3.2 Field Trapping Experiment

Chemicals

Synthetic *EE*10,12-16:Ald (isomeric purity 97.8%), *EE*10,12-16:OH (97.9%), and *E*10-16:Ald (>99.9%) were obtained from the Biocontrol Research Laboratories, India.

Preparation of Lures

Pheromone lures were prepared at IGZ in Germany. Rubber septa (Pherobank BV) were incubated in hexane (≥98%, SupraSolv, Merck) two times overnight and dried at room temperature in the fume hood. Stock solutions were prepared by dissolving a defined amount of each compound in hexane. The component ratios were adjusted according to the natural composition of the female gland extracts from Taiwan and Thailand as determined by GC–FID (Tab. 1; see also section 3.4.1). An equivalent amount of 2,6-di-tert-butyl-4-methylphenol (butylated hydroxytoluene, BHT; VWR) was added to the pheromone solution as antioxidant. As negative control, septa were baited only with 231 µg BHT. Blend compositions were confirmed by GC–MS, and 100 µl of pheromone solution were applied to the cup of each rubber septum. The solvent was allowed to evaporate under the fume hood. Loaded rubber septa were placed individually in crimp-capped vials, which were wrapped in aluminum foil and stored at −20°C until they were shipped to Taiwan and tested in the field.

Table 1 Amounts of the three pheromone components and BHT dissolved in 100 µl hexane and applied to each rubber septum for the Taiwan- and Thailand-lure.

Compound	Taiwan-lure [µg]	Thailand-lure [µg]
*EE*10,12-16:Ald	100	100
*EE*10,12-16:OH	88	148
*E*10-16:Ald	5	21
BHT	193	269

Field Tests

Unless otherwise noted, the field trapping experiments were conducted at the experimental site of AVRDC-The World Vegetable Center in Shanhua, Taiwan in April-May 2013 (weather station record; Tab. S3.1 and S3.2).

Experiment 1: Synthetic lures were tested in *M. vitrata*-infested yard long bean fields. Plant beds were covered with plastic film mulching (black) to control weed growth. Experiments were designed in randomized complete blocks with four replicates. Rubber septa were placed singly in the center of a sticky delta trap using wire. Traps were suspended from bamboo sticks using wire 180 cm above ground. The distance between individual traps was at least 15 m and the distance to the field edges was at least 4.5 m. Traps were placed in the field when flowering started. Lures were replaced and rotated weekly. Mated pairs and virgin males of *M. vitrata* were released daily to enhance crop infestation. Lures were removed after 2.5 weeks.

Experiment 2: The importance of the minor components was tested by comparing the Taiwan-lure with both or only one of the minor components (*EE*10,12-16:OH or *E*10-16:Ald) as attractant. The experimental set up was conducted according to experiment 1.

Experiment 3: The Taiwan-lure ($N = 3$) and a commercial lure (rubber septa; $N = 4$; Russell IPM Ltd, produced in 2012) were tested in *Sesbania cannabina* fields in the district of Meinong for five weeks. *S. cannabina* is used as a green manure and grown as cover crop. The traps were placed 30 cm above crop canopy and the distance between individual traps was at least 15 m. Lures were replaced and rotated weekly.

3.4 Results

3.4.1 Chemical Analysis of Pheromone Gland Extracts

The comparison of female gland extracts and the pheromone multicomponent standard using GC–FID revealed the presence of EE10,12-16:Ald, EE10,12-16:OH, and E10-16:Ald in samples of insects from Taiwan and Thailand. However, the quantification of E10-16:Ald was difficult due to an overlapping other compound. EE10,12-16:OH, which was previously described as minor compound, accounted for about 50% of the pheromone blend in both Asian populations (mean ±SE; Taiwan: 45.7% ±3.8%; Thailand: 55% ±2.9%) when samples were analyzed within three days after extraction (Fig. 1). The major pheromone component EE10,12-16:Ald accounted for 51.9% ±3.4% and 37.2% ±3.3% in samples from Taiwan and Thailand, respectively. Interestingly, the relative percentages of EE10,12-16:Ald and E10-16:Ald in gland extracts differed significantly between females from Taiwan (N = 31) and Thailand (N = 27) (MANOVA; EE10,12-16:Ald: P = 0.0128; E10-16:Ald: P = <0.0001). E10-16:Ald represented a significantly lower relative percentage in the pheromone ratio of Taiwanese females (2.5% ±1.2%) compared to females from Thailand (7.8% ±0.5%). Conversely, the relative percentage of EE10,12-16:Ald was higher in gland extracts of Taiwanese females (51.9% ±3.4%) compared to females from Thailand (37.2% ±3.3%).

Our chemical analyses further suggested that long sample storage time (> 3 days) might affect the pheromone compound ratios detected in the samples. We analyzed this effect using a set of gland extracts from Thai females which were stored for a short (< 3 days), middle (4-7 days), and long (> 8 days) time after extraction at -80°C (Fig. 2). The comparison of different storage times revealed an increased relative percentage of EE10,12-16:Ald when samples were stored more than one week before GC–FID analysis (short: 37.2% ±3.3%; long: 87.8% ±2.0%; MANOVA, P = <0.0001). In contrast, the percentage of EE10,12-16:OH decreased significantly and was detectable only in traces after one week (short: 55% ±2.9%; long: 3.2% ±0.5%; MANOVA, P = <0.0001). The proportion of E10-16:Ald did not vary significantly (MANOVA, P = 0.5557).

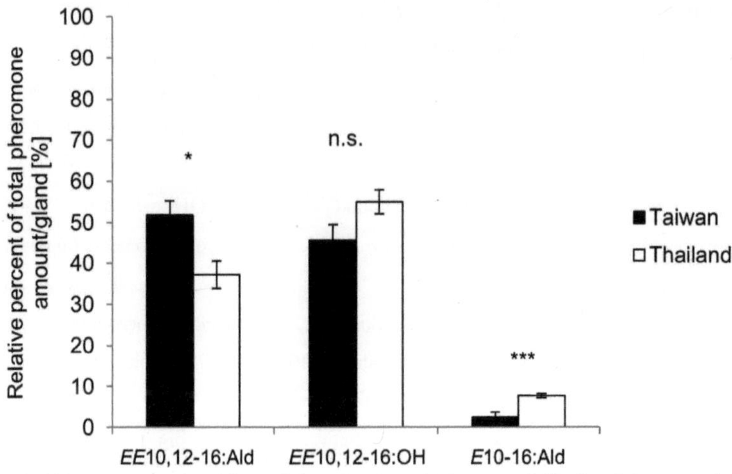

Figure 1 Pheromone composition of females from Taiwan and Thailand (storage time <3 days) (MANOVA, mean ± SE, N = 27-31), n.s.: not significant, * $P < 0.05$, *** $P < 0.001$.

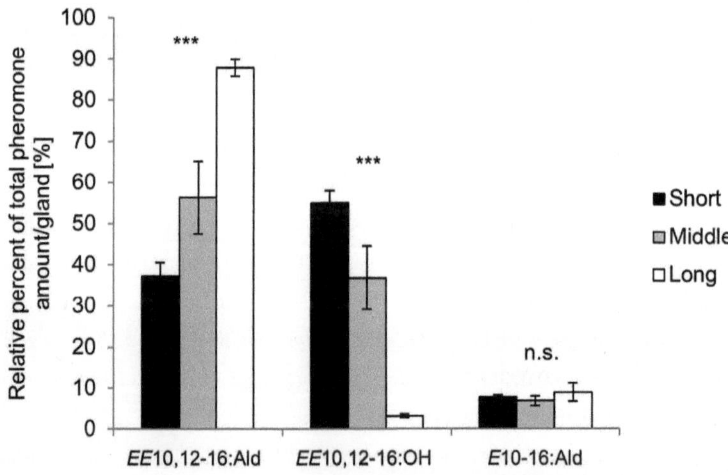

Figure 2 Effect of storage time on pheromone blend composition in gland extracts from Thailand females analyzed by GC–FID (short: ≤ 3 days, middle: 4 to 7 days, long ≥ 8 days) (MANOVA, mean ± SE, N = 14-27), n.s.: not significant, *** $P < 0.001$.

3.4.2 Field Trapping Experiment

Delta traps baited with the Taiwan- or Thailand-lure did not attract *M. vitrata* males in yard long bean and *S. cannabina* fields in Taiwan (Tab. 2–4). Only few *M. vitrata* were caught in traps in addition to various non-target lepidopterans. Also the Taiwan-lures with only one of both minor compounds (*EE*10,12-16:OH or *E*10-16:Ald), and the commercial lure from Russell IPM did not attract any *M. vitrata* males (Tab. 3 and 4).

Table 2 Field trapping experiment testing different pheromone blends in yard long bean fields for 2.5 weeks. Mean (± SE) trap catch per night of *M. vitrata* males and females and non-target lepidopterans ($N = 4$).

Lure	Non-target	Male	Female
Negative control	0.45 ± 0.11	0.01 ± 0.01	0
Taiwan-blend	0.61 ± 0.08	0	0
Thailand-blend	0.42 ± 0.13	0	0.01 ± 0.01

Table 3 Field trapping experiment testing the importance of the minor compounds in pheromone lures in yard long bean fields for 2.5 weeks. Mean (± SE) trap catch per night of *M. vitrata* males and females and non-target lepidopterans ($N = 4$).

Lure	Non-target	Male	Female
Taiwan-blend	0.71 ± 0.51	0	0.01 ± 0.01
*EE*10,12-16:Ald + *E*10-16:Ald	0.65 ± 0.32	0	0
*EE*10,12-16:Ald + *EE*10,12-16:OH	0.88 ± 0.64	0	0

Table 4 Field trapping experiment testing the Taiwan-blend ($N = 3$) and a commercial lure (Russell IPM, produced in 2012, $N = 4$) in *S. cannabina* fields in Meinong district for five weeks. Mean (± SE) trap catch per night of *M. vitrata* males and females and non-target lepidopterans.

Lure	Non-target	Male	Female
Taiwan-blend	0.37 ± 0.11	0.01 ± 0.01	0.01 ± 0.01
Russell IPM lure	0.66 ± 0.14	0	0.01 ± 0.01

3.5 Discussion

Our GC–FID analyses indicated the presence of EE10,12-16:Ald, EE10,12-16:OH, and E10-16:Ald in gland extracts of *M. vitrata* females from both Asian regions. Surprisingly, pheromone blends of females from Taiwan and Thailand contained similar amounts of EE10,12-16:OH and EE10,12-16:Ald. In previous studies, the proportion of EE10,12-16:OH in the pheromone blend was much lower compared to EE10,12-16:Ald (100%): 3–4% in a pooled gland extract of an insect population from Ghana (Adati and Tatsuki 1999), 2–5% in a pooled gland extract from a mixed *M. vitrata* population from Benin, Nigeria, Taiwan, and India (Downham et al. 2003), and 0.7% and 12.1% in Chinese populations from Huazhou and Wuhan, respectively (Lu et al. 2013).

The relative percentage of E10-16:Ald was significantly higher in gland extracts of Thai females than in Taiwanese females (7.8% and 2.5%, respectively). In initial studies, E10-16:Ald could not be detected in gland extracts of females from different populations by GC–MS (Adati and Tatsuki 1999; Downham et al. 2003). However, Lu et al. (2013) found 10.3% and even 79.5% of E10-16:Ald compared to EE10,12-16:Ald (100%) in female gland extracts from two different Chinese *M. vitrata* populations.

In our experiments, the pheromone blend composition in gland extracts was significantly affected by storage times longer than one week at -80°C. Especially the relative percentage of EE10,12-16:OH in samples decreased drastically. No other studies specifically addressed the chemical stability of pheromone compounds in gland extracts of *M. vitrata*. However, Lu et al. (2013) analyzed single gland extracts immediately by GC–MS. Therefore, pheromone ratios in samples were most likely not affected by different storage times in their study.

Based on the results of our chemical analyses we tested synthetic lures mimicking the pheromone blend composition of females from Taiwan and Thailand as attractants in the field in Taiwan. These pheromone blends differed considerably from the one attracting the insect population from Benin (100:5:5-blend) (Downham et al. 2003), which might be the reason for the failure of the 100:5:5-blend in Asia. Also in field trapping experiments with two geographically different populations in China, most *M. vitrata* males were caught in traps baited with the pheromone blend corresponding to the local population (Lu et al. 2013). However, in our experiments, neither the Taiwan-blend, nor any other blend attracted *M. vitrata* males in the field in Taiwan. One possible explanation for the failure of pheromone lures in field trapping experiments is photoisomerization of compounds containing conjugated diene systems, such as *EE*10,12-16:Ald and *EE*10,12-16:OH, induced by sunlight (Cork 2004). For example, the addition of an isomer (*EZ*10,12-16:Ald) to the major pheromone component *EE*10,12:16Ald of *Earias vittella* F. significantly reduced trap catches in field bioassays (Cork et al. 1988). In behavioral bioassays, the addition of *EZ*10,12-16:Ald to *EE*10,12-16:Ald also reduced attraction of *M. vitrata* males from Ghana (Adati and Tatsuki 1999). Adati and Tatsuki (1999) also reported that *M. vitrata* males were more attracted to purified *EE*10,12-16:Ald (isomeric purity 99%) than to unpurified *EE*10,12-16:Ald (92%). In contrast, trap catches of *M. vitrata* males in field studies in Benin were not affected by different isomeric purities of *EE*10,12-16:Ald and *EE*10,12-16:OH ranging from 73% to >99% (Downham et al. 2004). In our study, the isomeric purity of synthetic pheromone compounds used to prepare pheromone lures was relatively high (*EE*10,12-16:Ald: 97.8%; *EE*10,12-16:OH: 97.9). In further field studies in Benin, pheromone lures were wrapped in aluminum foil to prevent photoisomerization (Downham et al. 2003, 2004), but there was no difference between male trap catches with shielded or unshielded pheromone dispensers (Downham et al. 2004). Generally, trap catches of *M. vitrata* males using synthetic lures are very low. In a period of eight weeks, the 100:5:5-blend attracted only a total of 33.1 (±2.4 SE) males per trap in Benin (Downham et al. 2003). In China, only 19.5 (±3.6 SD) males in total per trap were caught in four weeks (Lu et al. 2013). It might be possible that additional pheromone components are essential for the attraction of *M. vitrata* males.

In conclusion, although we found significant differences between pheromone blends of females from Taiwan and Thailand by GC–FID, the synthetic Taiwan blend was not attractive in field trapping experiments in Taiwan. However, the presence of stereoisomers or additional pheromone components could not be determined with this method. GC–MS analyses of gland extracts in comparison to all known stereoisomers of pheromone components may help to identify the correct ratio and potential additional pheromone components necessary for sexual attraction (addressed in Chapter 5). Moreover, the chemical stability of pheromone compounds applied to pheromone dispensers should be investigated under field conditions as well as storage conditions (addressed in Chapter 4).

3.6 Supplementary Material

Table S3.1 AVRDC-The World Vegetable Center: Weather Station Record April 2013

DATE	Atmospheric Pressure [hPa]		Humidity [%]			Air Temperature °C			Soil Temperature °C						Wind		Solar Intensity	Preci-pitation	Eva-poration
									10 cm			30 cm			Speed	Dir			
	Max	Min	Max	Min	Mean	Max	Min	Mean	Max	Min	Mean	Max	Min	Mean	m/s	deg	w-h/m2	mm	mm
01.04.2013	1013.0	1009.0	98.1	42.3	78.6	30.4	18.9	23.2	28.0	23.1	25.2	26.1	24.8	25.4	2.2	179.8	5199.8	0.0	4.6320
02.04.2013	1012.0	1008.0	100.0	40.6	74.7	30.8	19.6	24.2	29.0	23.8	26.2	26.7	25.1	25.8	2.5	221.1	6351.9	0.0	6.8080
03.04.2013	1011.0	1006.0	100.0	56.0	80.0	28.8	18.7	22.5	27.9	23.5	25.6	26.6	25.2	25.9	1.9	194.5	4092.8	7.8	1.8110
04.04.2013	1009.0	1003.0	100.0	40.1	85.2	32.9	19.1	23.5	27.9	22.8	25.3	26.2	24.7	25.4	1.8	124.0	5406.6	20.8	1.2480
05.04.2013	1005.0	1000.0	100.0	73.0	92.4	28.4	21.8	23.8	26.5	23.9	25.3	26.2	25.2	25.7	1.7	150.6	1464.9	30.2	0.3080
06.04.2013	1007.0	999.0	100.0	68.1	89.9	26.5	15.9	22.0	25.7	22.0	24.1	25.4	24.6	24.8	2.5	125.4	1306.8	31.4	3.3820
07.04.2013	1010.0	1005.0	88.1	41.7	58.6	23.3	14.0	17.9	23.5	20.3	21.9	24.8	23.1	23.7	2.3	123.2	2765.5	0.0	3.2240
08.04.2013	1011.0	1008.0	94.5	38.1	72.8	29.0	16.2	21.5	26.1	21.1	23.3	24.5	22.9	23.6	1.3	169.2	5538.8	0.0	3.3610
09.04.2013	1013.0	1010.0	99.8	43.1	83.6	29.4	18.5	21.6	26.5	22.4	24.1	24.8	23.8	24.3	2.2	112.6	4285.4	9.6	2.6740
10.04.2013	1014.0	1010.0	100.0	59.3	81.6	24.6	17.3	20.4	25.3	21.9	23.5	24.6	23.6	24.1	2.6	152.3	4745.3	0.0	2.1890
11.04.2013	1014.0	1011.0	94.2	58.5	78.8	25.0	17.0	20.3	24.6	22.0	23.2	24.4	23.6	23.9	1.9	128.6	3060.4	0.0	2.6530
12.04.2013	1015.0	1012.0	98.2	62.5	88.8	23.8	16.9	19.2	24.1	21.8	22.8	24.1	23.4	23.7	2.5	166.1	2808.1	0.0	2.5670
13.04.2013	1014.0	1011.0	98.8	57.7	86.1	26.0	16.8	20.6	24.2	21.6	22.8	23.8	23.1	23.4	1.0	193.1	2335.3	0.0	2.6360
14.04.2013	1012.0	1007.0	99.7	72.9	89.9	25.2	17.8	21.2	24.4	22.1	23.1	23.8	23.3	23.5	1.4	69.2	2392.9	0.0	1.9630
15.04.2013	1009.0	1006.0	100.0	44.9	76.5	30.1	17.3	23.3	26.6	21.8	24.0	24.8	23.1	23.7	1.1	224.4	6046.7	0.0	4.5390
16.04.2013	1008.0	1005.0	96.1	39.9	76.7	31.1	20.5	25.0	26.7	23.3	25.0	25.3	24.3	24.7	1.4	174.3	4448.5	0.0	4.5480
17.04.2013	1008.0	1006.0	99.0	40.5	77.5	32.6	20.7	25.5	27.8	23.6	25.6	25.8	24.6	25.1	1.1	218.0	4630.6	0.0	3.8000
18.04.2013	1009.0	1006.0	95.7	50.2	78.4	31.8	23.1	26.3	28.0	24.7	26.2	26.2	25.3	25.7	1.2	210.1	4500.2	0.0	4.1410
19.04.2013	1010.0	1006.0	98.8	57.7	89.0	28.7	22.7	25.0	27.5	25.1	26.2	26.2	25.7	26.0	1.1	237.5	2508.5	0.4	1.0420
20.04.2013	1011.0	1007.0	100.0	46.9	82.4	33.5	21.3	25.7	29.1	24.5	26.7	26.8	25.5	26.1	1.2	207.4	6053.9	0.8	4.2140
21.04.2013	1014.0	1009.0	99.9	62.6	83.5	26.8	18.6	22.4	27.7	24.7	26.4	26.8	26.0	26.4	2.4	237.9	4456.9	0.4	5.5630
22.04.2013	1014.0	1010.0	87.9	47.8	73.6	29.2	17.8	22.3	27.5	23.7	25.5	26.3	25.2	25.8	1.5	169.8	4357.6	0.0	4.0450
23.04.2013	1013.0	1009.0	90.7	28.4	66.3	33.9	21.1	26.0	28.6	24.3	26.3	26.7	25.4	25.9	1.4	162.4	6374.6	0.0	5.9330
24.04.2013	1013.0	1008.0	91.4	39.0	71.9	32.5	23.8	27.2	29.1	25.6	27.3	27.3	26.2	26.6	1.6	173.1	6338.5	0.0	6.0640
25.04.2013	1010.0	1008.0	98.5	44.1	78.5	31.6	22.1	25.4	28.9	26.0	27.4	27.4	26.6	27.0	2.2	199.6	5497.8	0.0	5.6650
26.04.2013	1012.0	1008.0	98.6	50.1	81.0	29.6	20.6	24.0	27.7	25.3	26.5	27.3	26.4	26.8	1.7	174.1	2990.5	3.6	1.5410
27.04.2013	1012.0	1009.0	99.9	81.6	94.4	24.0	20.7	21.9	26.0	24.5	25.2	26.7	25.6	26.0	0.8	121.5	1286.3	6.8	0.0190
28.04.2013	1012.0	1009.0	100.0	42.7	77.3	31.5	20.1	24.6	28.6	24.0	25.9	26.6	25.1	25.7	1.7	144.8	6834.7	0.6	2.6090
29.04.2013	1012.0	1009.0	100.0	32.6	72.6	33.6	19.6	25.7	29.3	24.6	26.9	27.2	25.8	26.4	1.2	241.7	7078.5	0.0	5.9020
30.04.2013	1010.0	1006.0	98.5	36.6	74.5	34.1	21.7	26.9	29.1	25.5	27.3	27.5	26.4	26.9	2.0	191.0	7201.4	0.0	6.4150
TOTAL	30337.0	30220.0	2926.4	1499.6	2395.1	878.6	579.8	699.0	811.8	703.3	754.9	776.7	743.5	757.8	51.0		132359.8	112.4	105.5
MEAN	1011.2	1007.3	97.5	50.0	79.8	29.3	19.3	23.3	27.1	23.4	25.2	25.9	24.8	25.3	1.7		4412.0	3.7	3.5165

Table S3.2 AVRDC-The World Vegetable Center: Weather Station Record May 2013

DATE	Atmospheric Pressure [hPa]		Humidity [%]			Air Temperature °C			Soil Temperature °C 10 cm			Soil Temperature °C 30 cm			Wind		Solar Intensity	Precipitation	Evaporation
	Max	Min	Max	Min	Mean	Max	Min	Mean	Max	Min	Mean	Max	Min	Mean	Speed m/s	Dir deg	w-h/m2	mm	mm
01.05.2013	1008.0	1003.0	98.1	54	79.5	29.6	20.1	24.5	28.8	25.9	27.3	27.5	26.8	27.2	2.2	200.1	5675.4	2.4	47.130
02.05.2013	1009.0	1006.0	98.9	79.1	88.2	23.9	20.8	22.2	27.1	24.9	25.6	27.3	26	26.5	1.1	174.1	1110.8	6.4	0.619
03.05.2013	1010.0	1007.0	100	67.5	88.8	27.5	20.5	23.1	26.8	24.4	25.4	26.1	25.5	25.8	1.3	117.7	2998.3	2.2	0.152
04.05.2013	1013.0	1008.0	100	47.7	81.1	31	20.3	24.4	27.5	24.4	25.9	26.3	25.5	25.9	1.3	209.1	3909.6	0	27.300
05.05.2013	1013.0	1010.0	98.7	52.8	79.6	31.2	21.5	25.6	28.6	24.9	26.7	26.9	25.9	26.3	1.8	242	5452.7	0	51.230
06.05.2013	1012.0	1009.0	96.2	57.3	82.1	30.1	22.4	25.6	28.3	25.8	27	27.1	26.4	26.7	1.8	226.2	4062	0	21.640
07.05.2013	1011.0	1008.0	95.8	50.6	81.1	31.4	22.3	25.6	28.4	25.7	27	27.2	26.5	26.8	1.6	203	4175.2	0	45.700
08.05.2013	1011.0	1008.0	98.3	51.6	79.8	31.8	22.5	26	28.5	25.8	27.1	27.3	26.6	26.9	1.2	246	3885.5	0.4	31.610
09.05.2013	1010.0	1007.0	96.2	32	75.5	36.3	22.3	27	29.2	25.8	27.5	27.7	26.7	27.1	1	185.3	5286.6	0	48.220
10.05.2013	1009.0	1005.0	95.7	38	72.7	34.9	23.3	28.2	29.7	26.5	28.1	28.2	27.1	27.6	1.8	174.4	6804.9	0	74.440
11.05.2013	1008.0	1004.0	87.4	37.5	73.3	33.8	24.4	27.6	29.6	27.1	28.3	28.4	27.6	28	1.6	209.4	5633.7	0	63.570
12.05.2013	1008.0	1005.0	96.4	73.5	89.3	28.7	24.3	25.7	28.8	26.7	27.6	28.4	27.4	27.8	1.1	152.9	1741.5	11.2	0.324
13.05.2013	1007.0	1005.0	96.5	55.1	82.5	31.6	23.5	26.9	28.9	26.3	27.4	27.8	27	27.3	1.4	127.8	4964.1	2.2	0.164
14.05.2013	1007.0	1005.0	97.9	47.8	78.9	33.6	22.3	27.1	29.5	26.3	27.9	28.2	27.1	27.6	1.3	169	5971.3	0	53.760
15.05.2013	1007.0	1004.0	94.9	32.1	66.8	55.2	1	28.4	29.7	26.8	28.3	28.5	27.6	28	2.3	168.7	6710.4	0	84.630
16.05.2013	1007.0	1004.0	95.2	68.2	84.7	30.2	25.3	26.8	28.9	27.2	27.9	28.5	27.7	28.1	1.8	152.5	2796.9	10	0.598
17.05.2013	1007.0	1005.0	100	48.7	84	33.8	23	26.9	28.1	25	26.8	28	26.3	27.1	1.3	188.4	2729.9	71.8	0.832
18.05.2013	1007.0	1004.0	98.7	79.9	91.1	28.7	24.7	26.4	27.9	26.2	27.1	27.4	27	27.2	1.5	148.3	1972.2	27.8	0.713
19.05.2013	1006.0	1003.0	99.1	76.1	92.1	28.9	23.2	25.7	27.7	25.8	26.7	27.3	26.8	27	1.7	148.7	1538.2	37	27.230
20.05.2013	1006.0	1003.0	99.8	59.3	88.9	32.8	23.5	26.2	28	25.4	26.7	27.2	26.4	26.8	1.5	142.8	3194	47	14.350
21.05.2013	1009.0	1003.0	99.5	51.4	82.5	31.7	23.6	26.9	27.7	25.4	26.5	27	26.3	26.6	1.9	174.7	3124.8	16.6	0.176
22.05.2013	1007.0	1004.0	95.2	47.6	80.8	33.4	24.3	26.8	27.9	25.8	26.8	27.1	26.6	26.9	2.2	165	3685.4	4.4	20.940
23.05.2013	1009.0	1006.0	95.8	44	79	33.2	24.7	27.4	28.7	26	27.2	27.5	26.7	27	1.3	161.6	4125.4	0.2	17.730
24.05.2013	1009.0	1006.0	95.8	41.4	76.5	33.9	24.3	27.9	29.9	26.5	28.1	28.3	27.2	27.6	1.5	226.1	6913.2	0	74.570
25.05.2013	1010.0	1007.0	98	43.6	76.8	34.8	23.8	27.6	30	27.1	28.6	28.6	27.7	28.1	1.2	204.3	6625.3	0	62.020
26.05.2013	1009.0	1007.0	96	39.4	70.6	34.4	23.5	28.1	30	27.3	28.7	28.8	28	28.4	1.3	181.6	5785.6	0	68.930
27.05.2013	1009.0	1006.0	89.5	37.5	64.7	34.6	23.8	29	30.3	27.3	28.7	29.1	28.1	28.5	2	189.1	7473.1	0	83.220
28.05.2013	1011.0	1007.0	93.3	45.2	71.7	33.7	24.7	28.3	29.4	27.8	28.6	29	28.4	28.6	1.2	160.5	3923.1	10.4	0.951
29.05.2013	1012.0	1009.0	93.9	37.5	68.1	34.7	25.2	29.8	30.9	27.8	29.2	29.4	28.3	28.7	1.3	190.3	7723.7	0	71.310
30.05.2013	1012.0	1008.0	93.7	37.3	71.9	35	24.4	29	31	28.2	29.7	29.6	28.9	29.2	1.3	169.2	6598.4	0	69.260
31.05.2013	1010.0	1007.0	95.6	33.3	67.2	35.6	24.2	29.3	31.3	28.1	29.8	29.9	28.9	29.4	1.2	205.1	8130.3	0	79.440
TOTAL	31283	31183	2990.1	1567	2450.1	1019.9	697.6	830.2	896.8	813.9	854.3	865.4	838.8	850.6	46.9		144721.4	250	1183520.0
MEAN	1009.1	1005.9	96.5	50.5	79	32.9	22.5	26.8	28.9	26.3	27.6	27.9	27.1	27.4	1.5		4668.4	8.1	38.178

4 Chapter IV

Chemical stability of *Maruca vitrata* sex pheromone compounds on different dispensers under storage and simulated field conditions

Results communicated at

- 48. Gartenbauwissenschaftliche Jahrestagung 2013, Rheinische Friedrich-Wilhelms-Universität Bonn. (Schläger S, Ulrichs C, Beran F, Schreiner M und Mewis I. (2013) Optimierung der Fängigkeit von *Maruca vitrata* durch Pheromonfallen. BHGL – Schriftenreihe Band 29, 2013, p. 28)

- International Chemical Ecology Conference, Melbourne Convention & Exhibition Centre (Schläger S, Ulrichs C, Beran F, Groot AT, Srinivasan R, Lin M-Y, Yule S, Bhanu KRM, Schreiner M and Mewis I (2013) Pheromone blend variation of *Maruca vitrata* and investigations on pheromone stability for refining lures in Southeast Asia. Book of abstracts p.178)

4.1 Abstract

To date, synthetic pheromone lures comprised of (*E,E*)-10,12-hexadecadienal, (*E,E*)-10,12-hexadecadienol and (*E*)-10-hexadecenal for monitoring of the legume pod borer *Maruca vitrata* attracted only a few or no insects at all. One possible reason for low attractiveness of synthetic lures is the isomerization or chemical degradation of pheromone compounds particularly under field conditions. Based on re-extraction of pheromone dispensers, we analyzed the chemical stability of (*E,E*)-10,12-hexadecadienal, (*E,E*)-10,12-hexadecadienol, and (*E*)-10-hexadecenal loaded together with butylated hydroxytoluene as antioxidant on rubber septa or polyethylene vials under storage conditions and simulated field conditions by gas chromatography – mass spectrometry. Our results showed that all compounds were stable on both dispenser types and tested conditions.

4.2 Introduction

The larvae of *Maruca vitrata* cause severe damage on commercially important legume crops throughout the tropics (Sharma et al. 1999). In the past, many efforts were made to develop synthetic pheromone lures for monitoring *M. vitrata* in the field. Field trapping experiments in Benin and China confirmed the attractiveness of different blends of (*E,E*)-10,12-hexadecadienal (*EE*10,12-16:Ald), (*E,E*)-10,12-hexadecadienol (*EE*10,12-16:OH), and (*E*)-10-hexadecenal (*E*10-16:Ald), but overall trap catches were very low (Adati and Tatsuki 1999; Downham et al. 2003; Lu et al. 2013). For example, in eight weeks, only 33.1 (±2.4 SE) males were caught per trap in total in Benin (Downham et al. 2003). In China, only 19.5 (±3.6 SD) males in total per trap were caught in four weeks (Lu et al. 2013). Lu et al. (2013) used exclusively rubber septa as pheromone dispensers, whereas Downham et al. (2003) used rubber septa as well as polyethylene (PE) vials. Although field studies in Benin revealed that the synthetic blend attracted slightly more *M. vitrata* males at a dosage of 0.1 mg from PE vials than from rubber septa, this difference was not significant (Downham et al. 2003). In all field studies, delta traps were used as trap design (Downham et al. 2003; Lu et al. 2013).

Isomeric purity and chemical stability of synthetic pheromone components are crucial factors influencing lure efficiency (Cork 2004). Aldehydes, such as *EE*10,12-16:Ald and *E*10-16:Ald, are known to react with atmospheric oxygen to form carboxylic acids (Stevens 1998). To prevent oxidation, synthetic pheromone lures are combined with antioxidants in a ratio of 1:1, for example with butylated hydroxytoluene (BHT) (Cork 2004). Field studies with the cotton leaf-roller *Haritalodes derogata* (Lepidoptera: Crambidae) revealed that trap catches increased considerably when BHT was added to the pheromone lure comprising of *EZ*10,12-16:Ald and *EE*10,12-16:Ald (Himeno and Honda 1992). The lures for trapping *M. vitrata* in Benin were also loaded with an equivalent weight of BHT (Downham et al. 2003), whereas lures for field studies in China were not prepared including antioxidants (Lu et al. 2013).

Furthermore, *EE*10,12-16:Ald as well as *EE*10,12-16:OH contain conjugated double bonds which may be susceptible to photoisomerization induced by sunlight (Cork 2004). For example, decreased trap catches of *Earias vittella* and *E. insulana* (Lepidoptera: Nolidae) were observed for consecutive nights when lures were exposed to sunlight during the day (Cork et al. 1988). Subsequent chemical analysis revealed isomerization of the pheromone component *EE*10,12-16:Ald. However, when lures were removed from the field in the daytime, *E. vittella* males were successfully trapped for eleven consecutive days. For

M. vitrata, Adati and Tatsuki (1999) observed that males from Ghana were more attracted to purified *EE*10,12-16:Ald (isomeric purity 99%) than to unpurified *EE*10,12-16:Ald (92%) in behavioral assays in the laboratory. In contrast, trap catches of *M. vitrata* males in field trapping experiments in Benin were not affected by isomeric purities of *EE*10,12-16:Ald and *EE*10,12-16:OH ranging from 73 to >99% (Downham et al. 2004).

To prevent degradation of pheromone components by ultraviolet (UV) light, UV-stabilizers are loaded additionally on pheromone dispensers (Jones 1998). However, synthetic lures for trapping *M. vitrata* were not merged with UV-stabilizers, such as 2-hydroxy-4-methoxybenzophenone (Ideses and Shani 1988), in field studies in Benin and China (Downham et al. 2003; Lu et al. 2013). This indicates that low isomeric purity may be at least partially responsible for the low attractiveness of synthetic pheromone lures for *M. vitrata*. However, wrapping pheromone dispensers with aluminum foil to prevent direct solar irradiation did not increase trap catches of *M. vitrata* males in Benin (Downham et al. 2004).

In this study, we addressed the possible fate of synthetic sex pheromone compounds of *M. vitrata* on rubber septa and PE vials as pheromone dispensers under simulated field conditions as well as under storage conditions.

4.3 Methods and Materials

Chemicals

Synthetic *EE*10,12-16:Ald (isomeric purity 97.5%), *EE*10,12-16:OH (92.2%), and *E*10-16:Ald ($\geq$99.9%) were obtained from Biocontrol Research Laboratories (BCRL) in Bangalore, India.

Lure Preparation

Two dispenser types were used for the pheromone stability test: red rubber septa (10×20 mm, Wheaton) (Fig. 1a) and PE vials (Pherobank BV) (Fig. 1b). For cleaning, dispensers were immersed in hexane ($\geq$98%, SupraSolv, Merck) overnight (Fig. 1c). The remaining solvent was discarded and dispensers were dried at room temperature in a fume hood. Based on GC–FID analyses of Taiwanese female gland extracts (see section 3.4.1), 100 µg *EE*10,12-16:Ald, 88 µg *EE*10,12-16:OH, and 5 µg *E*10-16:Ald in 100 µl hexane ($\geq$98%, SupraSolv, Merck) were loaded per dispenser. Additionally, an equivalent weight of butylated hydroxytoluene (193 µg; BHT; VWR) was added as antioxidant. Stock solutions of all compounds were prepared by dissolving a defined amount of each pure compound in hexane ($\geq$98%, SupraSolv, Merck). Six technical replicates were prepared for each time point. As negative control, dispensers were loaded only with 193 µg BHT dissolved in 100 µl hexane. Three technical replicates were prepared for each time point.

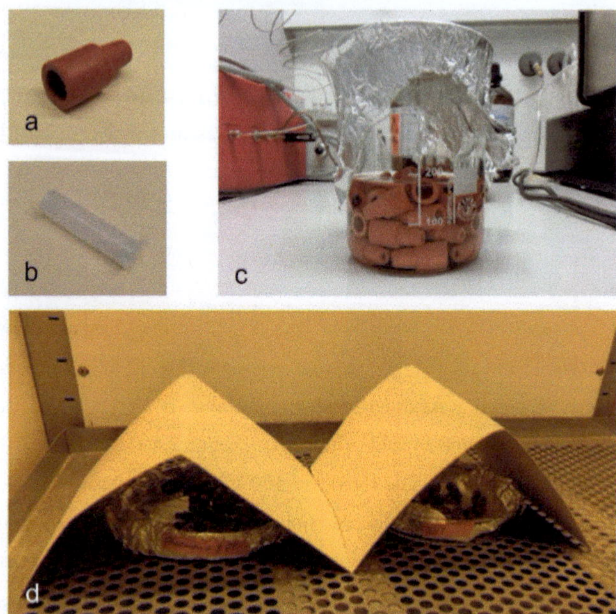

Figure 1 Rubber septa (a), polyethylene vials (b), rubber septa immersed in hexane (c) and loaded rubber septa shielded with paper in the climate chamber (d).

Analysis of Pheromone Stability under Storage Conditions

To analyze pheromone stability under storage conditions, pheromone dispensers were placed individually in crimp-capped vials which were afterwards wrapped in aluminum foil. The vials were stored in the freezer at -20°C for up to six weeks. Lures were re-extracted every week. As reference for the initial amount, the pheromone dispensers were extracted immediately after loading of the pheromone compounds.

Analysis of Pheromone Stability under Simulated Field Conditions

Pheromone dispensers were kept in a climate controlled chamber (Vötsch) for one week at 25°C, 80% relative humidity, and 14 h light/10 h dark with 2000 µmol m^{-2} s^{-1} PAR light intensity. To simulate shading by a delta trap, lures were shielded using paper (Fig. 1d). Pheromone components and BHT were extracted from dispensers for seven subsequent days. To determine the initial loaded amount, lures were extracted immediately after loading the synthetic blend on the dispenser.

Extraction of Compounds from Dispensers and Analysis by Gas Chromatography – Mass Spectrometry (GC–MS)

Pheromone dispensers were placed individually in crimp-capped vials at room temperature and incubated overnight in hexane ($\geq$98%, SupraSolv, Merck) containing 10 µg of pentadecane ($\geq$99.8%, Sigma-Aldrich) as internal standard. According to the size of the pheromone dispenser, rubber septa were immersed in 5 ml hexane and PE vials in 10 ml hexane overnight. The solvent was afterwards reduced to about 1 ml under a stream of N_2 and extracts were analyzed using an Agilent 6890N gas chromatograph (GC) equipped with an OPTIMA 5–MS fused silica capillary column (30 m × 0.25 mm ID, 0.25 µm film, Macherey–Nagel) and coupled to an Agilent 5973 mass selective detector (MSD). One microliter per sample was injected in splitless mode using a GERSTEL MultiPurpose Sampler (MPS). The inlet temperature was 250°C. The carrier gas was helium at a constant flow rate (1 ml/min). The oven program was 70°C held for 1 min, increased at 10°C/min to 300°C, and held for 5 min. Quantification of the three pheromone components and BHT was performed by external calibration curves (1, 5, 10, 50, and 100 ng) for each compound. The amount of each compound was quantified by relating its peak area to the internal standard using the Agilent MSD ChemStation Data Analysis software. Since no synthetic standards of all authentic stereoisomers of *EE*10,12-16:Ald, *EE*10,12-16:OH, and *E*10-16:Ald were available at that time, we were not able to determine the absolute stereochemistry of isomerization products. Isomeric purities of the three pheromone compounds were determined by scanning the GC–MS data for peaks with the same mass spectra. The peak areas of all detected stereoisomers were summed up and the proportion of the starting compound was calculated.

Statistical Analysis

The amounts of pheromone extracted from dispensers under storage conditions and simulated field conditions were calculated in percent. Under storage conditions, the amount of pheromone determined after 1 week was set to 100% since the extracted amount was considerably higher compared to the amount extracted directly after loading. The freezing and thawing of the dispensers might affect the release of pheromone compounds from the matrix during extraction. Since dispensers used for testing simulated field conditions were not frozen, the extracted pheromone at day 0 (directly after loading the compound) was used as reference (100%) in this experiment. A linear regression of remaining percentages over time was calculated using Microsoft Excel 2010. Significant differences of the isomeric purity over time were analyzed using SAS 9.4 (SAS Institute 2001). Data was tested for normal distribution and homogeneity of variance. Depending on the result, the data were analyzed by one-way analysis of variance (ANOVA) followed by Tukey's range test or by the non-parametric Kruskal-Wallis test with Bonferroni correction for pairwise multiple comparisons.

4.4 Results

We did not detect the stereoisomer of E10-16:Ald by GC–MS analysis on rubber septa and PE vials, but we found two peaks with identical mass spectra of EE10,12-16:Ald (Fig. 2) and EE10,12-16:OH (Fig. 3), respectively, at different retention times.

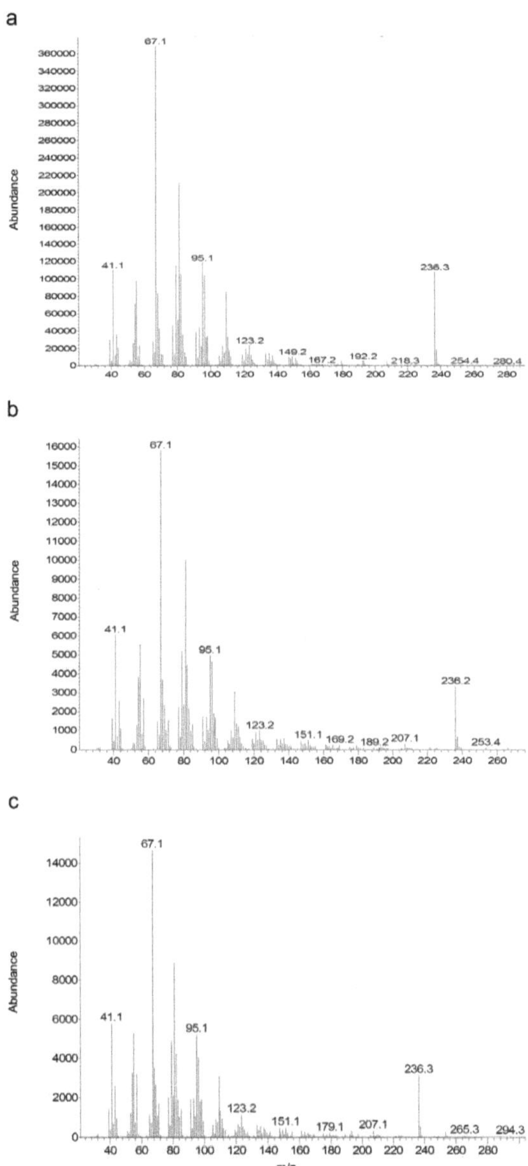

Figure 2 Representative EI mass spectra of *EE*10,12-16:Ald at the retention time of 15.696 min (a) and two unidentified isomers with identical mass spectra at 15.419 min (b) and 15.514 min (c).

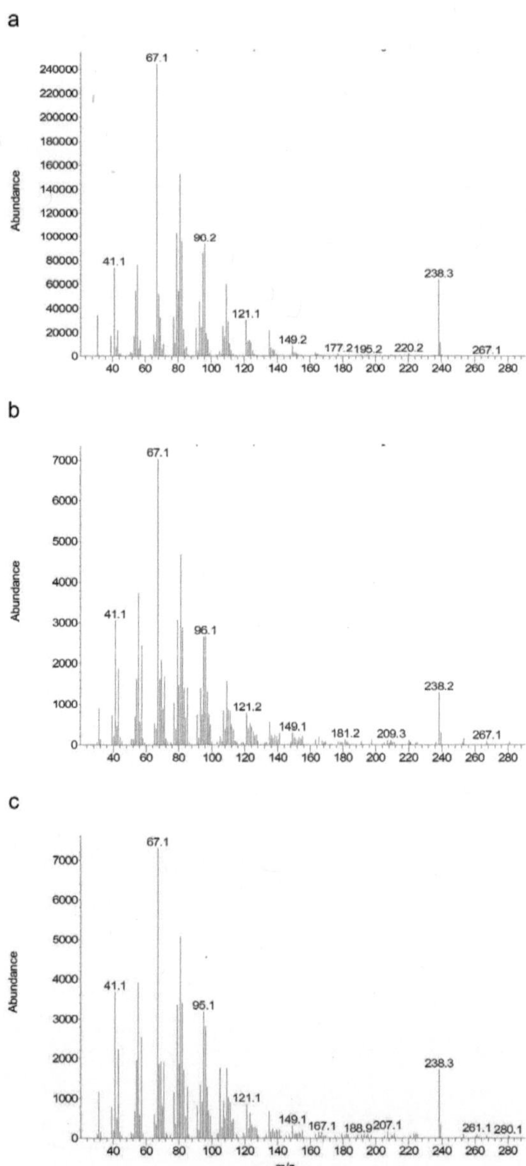

Figure 3 Representative EI mass spectra of *EE*10,12-16:OH at the retention time of 16.314 min (a) and two unidentified isomers with identical mass spectra at 16.076 min (b) and 16.155 min (c).

Analysis of Pheromone Stability under Storage Conditions

Higher amounts of *EE*10,12-16:Ald and *EE*10,12-16:OH were extracted from PE vials than from rubber septa under storage conditions at -20°C (Fig. 4a,b; Tab. S4.1). Extracted amounts of *E*10-16:Ald were usually higher from rubber septa than from PE vials. Interestingly, lower amounts of *EE*10,12-16:Ald and *EE*10,12-16:OH were extracted from rubber septa before storage at -20°C corresponding to control day 0 compared to pheromone amounts in the consecutive weeks (Fig. 4a; Tab. S4.1). On the other hand, the re-extracted amounts of both compounds from PE vials did not differ considerably before or after freezing (Fig 4b, Tab. S4.1). After six weeks at -20°C, 90% and 80% *EE*10,12-16:Ald (Fig. 5a,b), 94% and 90% *EE*10,12-16:OH (Fig. 5c,d), and 86% and 88% *E*10-16:Ald (Fig. 5e,f) were detected on rubber septa and PE vials, respectively. The isomeric purity of *EE*10,12-16:Ald and *EE*10,12-16:OH did not decrease significantly after six weeks (rubber septa: ANOVA, *EE*10,12-16:Ald: $P = 0.9936$, Kruskal Wallis test, *EE*10,12-16:OH: $P = 0.5658$; PE vials: Kruskal Wallis test, *EE*10,12-16:OH: $P = 0.9563$) (Tab. 1) with the exception of *EE*10,12-16:Ald on PE vials, where a significant decrease was detected after 6 weeks compared to week 0 (ANOVA, $P = 0.0005$).

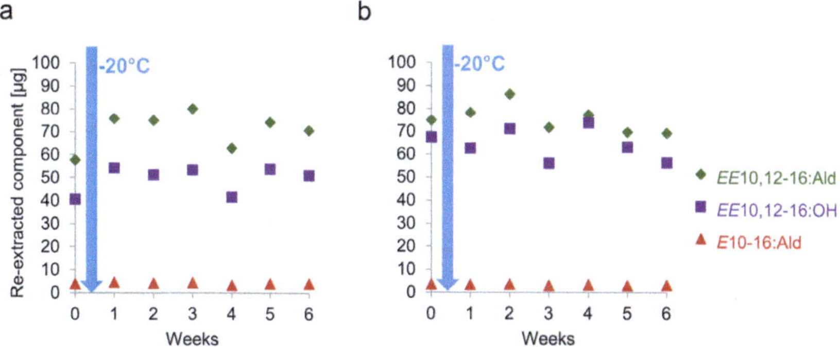

Figure 4 Amounts of re-extracted *EE*10,12-16:Ald, *EE*10,12-16:OH, and *E*10-16:Ald from rubber septa (a) and PE vials (b) under storage conditions. Blue arrows indicate the beginning of storage at -20°C.

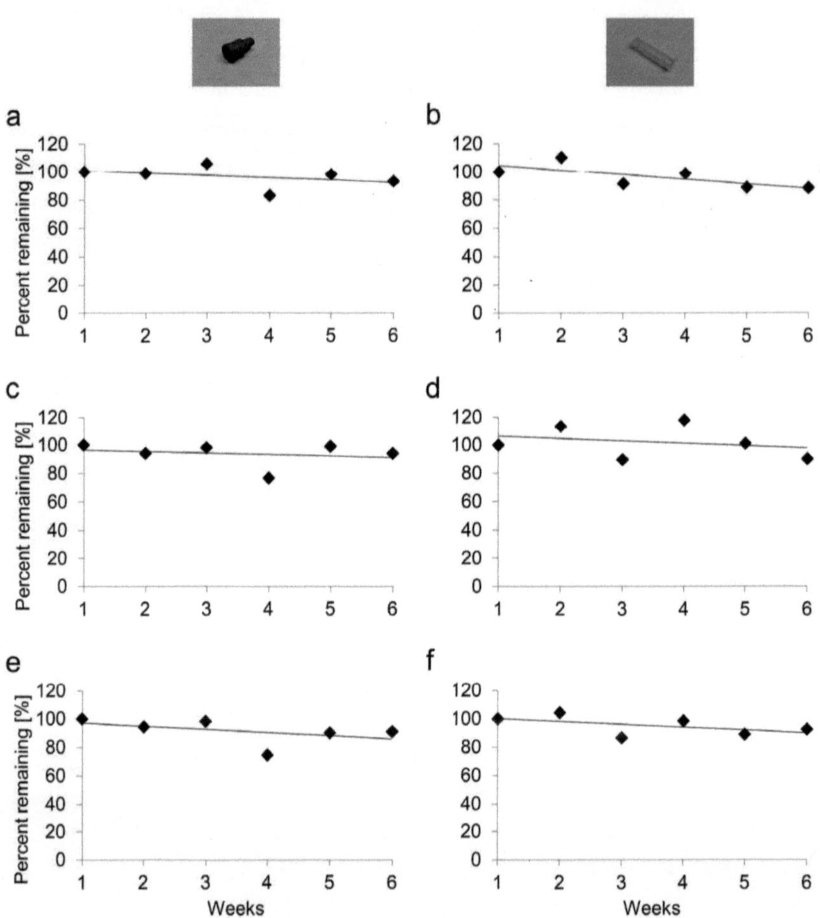

Figure 5 Remaining percentages of *EE*10,12-16:Ald (a,b), *EE*10,12-16:OH (c,d), and *E*10-16:Ald (e,f) from rubber septa and PE vials under storage conditions. The pheromone amounts extracted after one week were set to 100%.

Table 1 Isomeric purity (mean ±SD, $N = 6$) of *EE*10,12-16:Ald and *EE*10,12-16:OH extracted from rubber septa and PE vials for six consecutive weeks under storage conditions (mean ±SD, $N = 6$). Data with the same letter are not significantly different compared to week 0 according to ANOVA or Kruskal-Wallis test ($P \leq 0.05$).

Pheromone dispenser	Week	*EE*10,12-16:Ald [%]	*EE*10,12-16:OH [%]
Rubber septa	0	94.3 ± 0.3 a	98.25 ± 0.42 a
	1	95.08 ± 0.21 b	98.56 ± 0.51 a
	2	94.0 ± 0.42 a	96.9 ± 0.46 b
	3	93.79 ± 0.39 a	96.09 ± 0.66 b
	4	93.13 ± 0.34 b	95.74 ± 0.36 b
	5	94.92 ± 0.65 a	98.42 ± 0.9 a
	6	94.0 ± 1.13 a	97.49 ± 1.37 a
PE vial	0	95.67 ± 0.17 a	98.36 ± 0.37 a
	1	94.4 ± 0.83 b	96.94 ± 1.22 b
	2	94.69 ± 0.58 b	97.66 ± 0.76 a
	3	94.55 ± 0.47 b	97.9 ± 0.68 a
	4	95.96 ± 0.19 a	98.95 ± 0.34 a
	5	95.4 ± 0.59 a	98.83 ± 0.62 a
	6	94.25 ± 0.37 b	97.97 ± 0.48 a

Analysis of Pheromone Stability under Simulated Field Conditions

Pheromone dispensers as well as dispensers loaded only with BHT serving as control were placed together in the environment-controlled chamber. Our GC–MS analysis revealed no contaminations from emitted pheromone components on control dispensers. Again, higher amounts of *EE*10,12-16:Ald and *EE*10,12-16:OH were extracted from PE vials than from rubber septa under simulated field conditions (Fig. 6a,b; Tab. S4.2). The extracted amounts of *E*10-16:Ald were similar from both dispenser types. Under simulated field conditions, a release of *EE*10,12-16:Ald from rubber septa could not be determined (Fig. 7a), whereas 90% *EE*10,12-16:Ald remained on PE vials after seven days (Fig. 7b). 99.5% and 84% *EE*10,12-16:OH (Fig. 7c,d), and 97% and 83% *E*10-16:Ald (Fig. 7e,f) remained on rubber septa and PE vials, respectively. The isomeric purities of *EE*10,12-16:Ald and *EE*10,12-16:OH did not change significantly on rubber septa during one week (Kruskal Wallis test; *EE*10,12-16:Ald: $P = 0.9999$; *EE*10,12-16:OH: $P = 0.9952$) (Tab. 2), whereas the isomeric purities of both components were significantly lower after 4 days for *EE*10,12-16:Ald (ANOVA, $P = 0.049$) and after 5 days for *EE*10,12-16:OH (Kruskal Wallis test, $P = 0.0012$) on PE vials (Tab. 2).

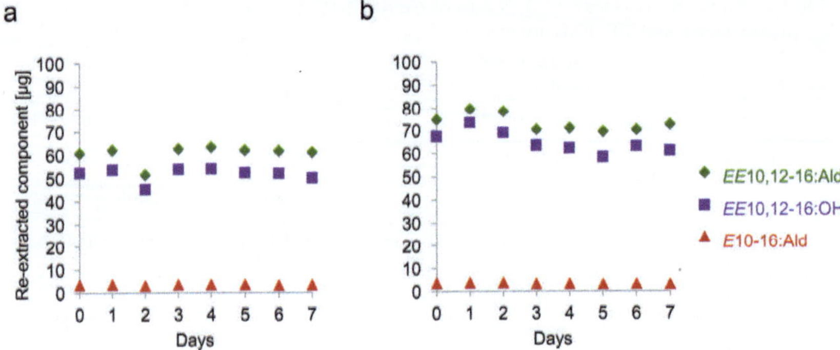

Figure 6 Amounts of extracted *EE*10,12-16:Ald, *EE*10,12-16:OH, and *E*10-16:Ald from rubber septa (a) and PE vials (b) under simulated field conditions in a climate controlled chamber (25°C, 80% relative humidity, and 14 h light/10 h dark with 2000 µmol m-2 s-1 PAR light intensity).

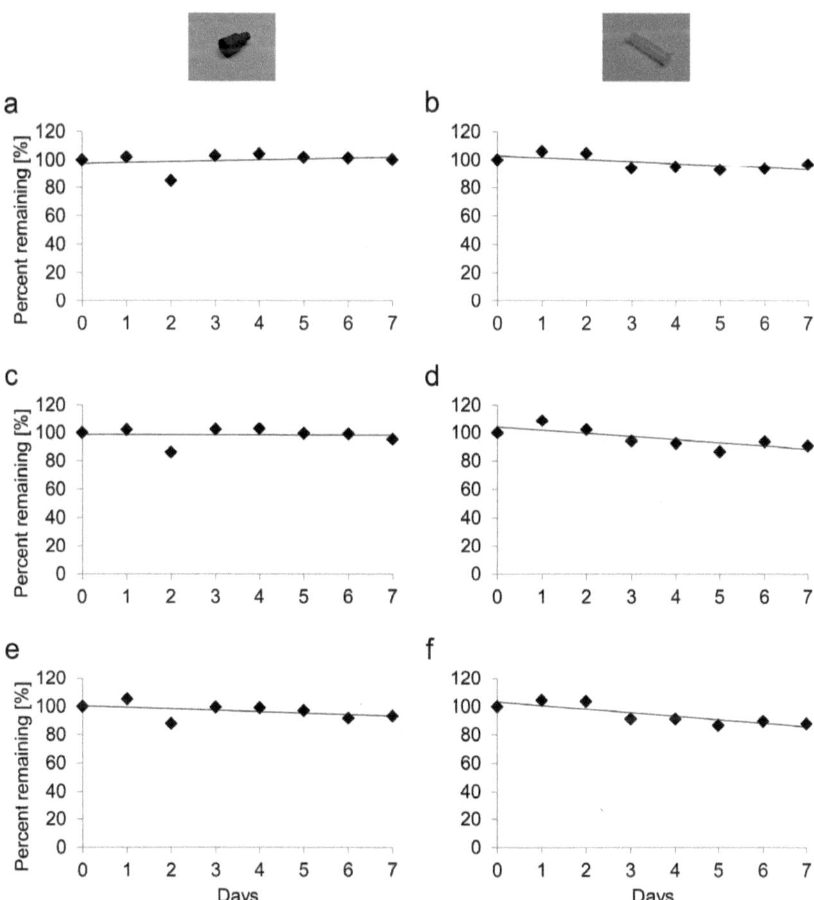

Figure 7 Remaining percentages of *EE*10,12-16:Ald (a,b), *EE*10,12-16:OH (c,d), and *E*10-16:Ald (e,f) from rubber septa and PE vials under simulated field conditions. The pheromone amounts extracted directly after application were set to 100%.

Table 2 Isomeric purity (mean ± SD, $N = 4 - 6$) of EE10,12-16:Ald and EE10,12-16:OH extracted from rubber septa and PE vials for seven consecutive days under simulated field conditions. Data with the same letter are not significantly different compared to day 0 according to ANOVA or Kruskal-Wallis test ($P \leq 0.05$).

Pheromone dispenser	Day	EE10,12-16:Ald [%]	EE10,12-16:OH [%]
Rubber septa	0	94.09 ± 0.39 a	98.24 ± 0.44 a
	1	93.84 ± 1.09 a	97.38 ± 1.32 a
	2	94.45 ± 0.35 a	97.61 ± 0.86 a
	3	93.76 ± 0.55 a	96.67 ± 1.31 a
	4	94.27 ± 0.39 a	97.88 ± 0.65 a
	5	94.19 ± 0.43 a	97.82 ± 0.84 a
	6	94.45 ± 0.24 a	97.98 ± 0.56 a
	7	94.23 ± 0.24 a	97.82 ± 0.36 a
PE vial	0	95.67 ± 0.17 a	98.36 ± 0.37 a
	1	95.52 ± 0.25 a	99.06 ± 0.25 a
	2	94.93 ± 0.51 a	98.27 ± 0.51 a
	3	94.96 ± 0.77 a	97.9 ± 1.16 a
	4	94.58 ± 0.41 b	97.12 ± 0.68 a
	5	94.58 ± 0.09 b	95.33 ± 0.65 b
	6	93.61 ± 1.12 b	95.4 ± 2.58 b
	7	93.97 ± 0.63 b	95.55 ± 1.11 b

4.5 Discussion

Under storage conditions, the release of *EE*10,12-16:Ald and *EE*10,12-16:OH was higher from PE vials compared to rubber septa over six weeks. Conversely, the release of *E*10-16:Ald was slightly higher from rubber septa than from PE vials. However, literature on the behavior of pheromone amounts under storage conditions is scarce. Cork and Farman reported that temperature affects synthetic pheromone amounts of *Helicoverpa armigera* on rubber septa in trilaminate aluminum sachets during a long storage time of six months (Cork 2004). A higher pheromone amount remained at 5°C (1.75 mg) compared to storage at 20°C (1.31 mg). The best result was obtained when lures were stored at -20°C (1.98 mg). Interestingly, extracted amounts of *EE*10,12-16:Ald and *EE*10,12-16:OH from rubber septa were higher before storage at -20°C. This effect was not detected on PE vials. This indicates that freezing possibly affects the physical properties of rubber septa leading for example to an increased porosity of the material. Consequently, higher amounts of *EE*10,12-16:Ald and *EE*10,12-16:OH could be extracted from rubber septa which had been frozen and stored at -20°C. Cork and Farman (Cork 2004) did not report an effect of the temperature on the properties of rubber septa when testing a standard lure for *Helicoverpa armigera* on this dispenser type. However, our finding needs further investigations because it is particularly important to evaluate the release rates of pheromone components from frozen rubber septa under subsequent field conditions. Rauscher and Arn (2001) performed field trapping experiments to investigate the influence of storage temperature (ambient, 4°C, and -18°C) on various synthetic pheromone lures on gray rubber caps after one and two years. The studies revealed that most of the lures were still attractive except of the one lure for *Lobesia botrana* (Lepidoptera: Tortricidae) stored at ambient conditions and at 4°C. This pheromone lure contained compounds with unsaturated double bonds and thus might be only stable at low temperatures (-18°C). In this study, we did not detect a strong decrease of the isomeric purities of *EE*10,12-16:Ald and *EE*10,12-16:OH on both dispenser types at -20°C. These results confirm that these sex pheromone components are stable under our storage conditions.

Under simulated field conditions, we expected a continuous decrease of pheromone components over time. However, in this study we did not determine the released pheromone amounts by collecting volatiles released from each dispenser. We again analyzed the remaining percentages of the pheromone components on each dispenser. Our results suggest a higher pheromone release rate from PE vials than from rubber septa since higher remaining percentages of pheromone could be detected after one week from rubber septa. In agreement with our results, Cork et al. (2001) reported higher remaining percentages of synthetic pheromone components of *Leucinodes orbonalis* (Lepidoptera: Pyralidae), (*E*)-11-hexadecenyl acetate (*E*11-16:Ac) and (*E*)-11-hexadecenol (*E*11-16:OH), on rubber septa (*E*11-16:Ac: 92%; *E*11-16:OH: 62%) than on PE vials (*E*11-16:Ac: 76%; *E*11-16:OH: 18%) under controlled conditions in a wind tunnel. However, we could not determine a decline of *EE*10,12-16:Ald on rubber septa under simulated field conditions in seven days. Cork et al. (2001) also performed solvent extraction from loaded pheromone dispensers to determine remaining percentages of the pheromone compounds. Their data revealed high variations between different extraction days. The decline of pheromone amounts from dispensers was determined over a longer time (40 days) compared to our study.

Under simulated field conditions, we did not detect any changes regarding the isomeric purity on rubber septa, whereas the isomeric purities of *EE*10,12-16:Ald and *EE*10,12-16:OH was significantly lower on PE vials after 4 and 5 days, respectively. In contrast to our results, Cork (2004) reported that the isomeric purity of *EE*11,13-16:Ald already decreased clearly on rubber septa after 3 days and decreased further after another five days. Conversely, *EE*11,13-16:Ald did not isomerize on PE vials after six days at room temperature under laboratory conditions.

Under both test conditions, we detected two stereoisomers of *EE*10,12-16:Ald and *EE*10,12-16:OH, respectively. Cork (2004) reported that *EZ*11,13-16:Ald and *ZE*11,13-16:Ald isomerized from *EE*11,13-16:Ald on rubber septa and PE vials in a stability test at room temperature under laboratory conditions (Cork 2004). The formation of *ZZ*11,13-16:Ald was not detected during six (PE vials) or eight (rubber septa) days under these conditions. Moreover, our findings indicate that isomerization of *EE*10,12-16:Ald apparently already occurred during loading of pheromone dispensers. Cork (2004) reported similar findings comparing the isomeric purities of *EE*11,13-16:Ald in the initial solution (97.49% and 97.57%) with the directly re-extracted aldehyde from both dispenser types (rubber septa: 89.35% and 90.9%; PE vials: 94.79% and 95.66%). Regarding the results for the rubber septa, it might be possible that rubber substrates caused isomerization. Vrkoč et al. (1988) reported that curing of rubber septa by exposure to sulfur led to isomerization of (*E,Z*)-7,9-dodecadienol acetate and (*E,E*)-8,10-dodecadienol acetate.

Summing up our results, we found that *EE*10,12-16:Ald, *EE*10,12-16:OH, and *E*10-16:Ald when combined with BHT remained stable on rubber septa and polyethylene vials under storage conditions for six weeks and under simulated field conditions for seven days. The correct ratio of the pheromone components is crucial to design efficient lures (Baker 2008). Therefore, the pheromone release should be determined from both dispenser types by performing headspace volatile collections. With this technique, the actual released quantities as well as the ratio of pheromone compounds can be evaluated.

4.6 Supplementary Material

Table S4.1 Amounts [µg] of extracted *EE*10,12-16:Ald, *EE*10,12-16:OH, and *E*10-16:Ald from rubber septa and PE vials under storage conditions (mean ±SD, $N = 6$).

Pheromone dispenser	Week	*EE*10,12-16:Ald	*EE*10,12-16:OH	*E*10-16:Ald
Rubber septa	0	57.73 ±2.95	40.59 ±1.97	3.91 ±0.41
	1	75.71 ±2.17	54.34 ±1.66	4.57 ±0.13
	2	74.97 ±1.37	51.24 ±0.96	4.31 ±0.21
	3	80.19 ±4.17	53.34 ±2.41	4.50 ±0.23
	4	62.96 ±1.33	41.66 ±0.86	3.41 ±0.14
	5	74.28 ±0.92	53.90 ±1.02	4.12 ±0.10
	6	70.67 ±0.95	51.18 ±1.02	4.17 ±0.23
PE vials	0	75.02 ±2.65	67.46 ±1.69	3.70 ±0.12
	1	78.25 ±2.49	62.60 ±2.14	3.49 ±0.08
	2	86.39 ±1.38	71.16 ±2.58	3.64 ±0.11
	3	71.75 ±1.03	56.19 ±1.04	3.02 ±0.6
	4	77.45 ±2.34	73.87 ±2.65	3.43 ±0.10
	5	69.72 ±0.84	63.23 ±1.19	3.11 ±0.07
	6	69.22 ±0.70	56.48 ±1.76	3.23 ±0.10

Table S4.2 Amounts [μg] of extracted *EE*10,12-16:Ald, *EE*10,12-16:OH, and *E*10-16:Ald from rubber septa and PE vials under simulated field conditions (mean ±SD, *N* = 4-6).

Pheromone dispenser	Day	*EE*10,12-16:Ald	*EE*10,12-16:OH	*E*10-16:Ald
Rubber septa	0	60.81 ±3.44	52.47 ±2.59	3.55 ±0.14
	1	62.22 ±1.71	53.70 ±1.46	3.73 ±0.14
	2	51.61 ±1.54	45.16 ±1.00	3.12 ±0.20
	3	62.70 ±1.99	53.83 ±1.81	3.54 ±0.15
	4	63.49 ±2.12	54.02 ±1.87	3.52 ±0.11
	5	62.09 ±2.50	52.32 ±2.11	3.45 ±0.10
	6	61.74 ±2.22	52.08 ±1.77	3.26 ±0.14
	7	61.09 ±1.98	50.09 ±1.03	3.31 ±0.12
PE vials	0	75.02 ±2.65	67.46 ±1.69	3.68 ±0.13
	1	79.76 ±2.30	73.57 ±2.83	3.85 ±0.06
	2	78.70 ±1.38	69.21 ±1.81	3.83 ±0.02
	3	70.49 ±1.58	63.60 ±1.68	3.36 ±0.07
	4	71.25 ±1.51	62.41 ±1.52	3.36 ±0.09
	5	69.58 ±1.86	58.51 ±2.30	3.20 ±0.07
	6	70.39 ±2.07	63.28 ±1.84	3.30 ±0.11
	7	72.63 ±3.01	61.26 ±2.47	3.24 ±0.10

5 Chapter V

Pheromone Blend Analysis and Cross-Attraction among Populations of *Maruca vitrata* from Asia and West Africa

Published in Schläger S, Beran F, Groot AT, Ulrichs C, Veit D, Paetz C, Karumuru BRM, Srinivasan R, Schreiner M and Mewis I. (2015) Pheromone blend analysis and cross-attraction among populations of *Maruca vitrata* from Asia and West Africa. Journal of Chemical Ecology 41 (12): 1155-1162. DOI 10.1007/s10886-015-0653-z

5.1 Abstract

The legume pod borer, *Maruca vitrata*, is a pantropical pest on leguminous crops. (*E,E*)-10,12-Hexadecadienal, (*E,E*)-10,12-hexadecadienol, and (*E*)-10-hexadecenal were described previously as sex pheromone components for this nocturnal moth. A blend of these components in a ratio of 100:5:5 attracted males in field trapping experiments in Benin, but not in Taiwan, Thailand, or Vietnam. This finding suggests geographic variation in the pheromone blend between Asian and West African populations of *M. vitrata*. We, therefore, determined the pheromone compositions of single pheromone glands of females from the three Asian regions and from Benin by gas chromatography—mass spectrometry. Additionally, we compared the responses of males from Taiwan and Benin to calling females and to gland extracts of females from both regions in laboratory no-choice and two-choice assays. Chemical analysis revealed the presence of (*E,E*)-10,12-hexadecadienal and (*E,E*)-10,12-hexadecadienol, as well as the absence of (*E*)-10-hexadecenal in all four populations. The relative amounts of the detected compounds did not vary significantly among the insect populations. The behavioral bioassays showed that Taiwanese and Beninese males were similarly attracted to females from both regions, as well as to their gland extracts. As a result, we did not find geographic variation in the sexual communication system of *M. vitrata* between West African and Asian insect populations.

Keywords: *Maruca vitrata*, sex pheromone, geographic variation, cross-attraction, (*E,E*)-10,12-hexadecadienal, (*E,E*)-10,12-hexadecadienol, (*E*)-10-hexadecenal, Lepidoptera Crambidae

5.2 Introduction

The legume pod borer, *Maruca vitrata* (F.) (Lepidoptera: Crambidae), causes severe damage on economically important leguminous crops throughout the tropics and subtropics (Sharma et al. 1999), and it is a major pest on yard long bean (*Vigna unguiculata* spp. *sesquipedalis*) in Thailand and Vietnam (Schreinemachers et al. 2014). This pest is controlled mainly by synthetic insecticides (Schreinemachers et al. 2014; Srinivasan et al. 2013), which are not very effective because the larvae are exposed only for a short time after hatching before they start feeding on plant organs internally (Sharma et al. 1999). Since development of insecticide resistance has been reported for *M. vitrata* (Ekesi 1999; Ulrichs et al. 2001), more specific and targeted use of insecticides is necessary to reduce its overuse. Pheromone traps are a valuable tool in crop protection for species-specific pest monitoring and are used to perform target-oriented control measures. The sex pheromone of *M. vitrata* has been studied for more than a decade. Initial work described (*E,E*)-10,12-hexadecadienal (*EE*10,12-16:Ald) as the major sex pheromone component and (*E,E*)-10,12-hexadecadienol (*EE*10,12-16:OH) as a minor component (Adati and Tatsuki 1999; Downham et al. 2003). However, *EE*10,12-16:OH did not increase male response of a *M. vitrata* population from Ghana in a behavioral bioassay (Adati and Tatsuki 1999), while males of a mixed insect population from Benin, Nigeria, India, and Taiwan approached *EE*10,12-16:Ald as an attractant in wind tunnel assays only when 5 % of *EE*10,12-16:OH was added (Downham et al. 2003). In addition to these two compounds, Downham et al. (2003) suggested the presence of a monounsaturated hexadecenal in gland extracts from the mixed *M. vitrata* population, based on gas chromatography—electroantennographic detection (GC/EAD). Comparing a range of synthetic monounsaturated hexadecenals, (*E*)-10-hexadecenal (*E*10-16:Ald) elicited the strongest electroantennographic (EAG) response from male antennae. Subsequent field trapping experiments revealed that a blend containing 100:5:5 *EE*10,12-16:Ald : *EE*10,12-16:OH : *E*10-16:Ald was the most attractive synthetic lure in Benin (Downham et al. 2003, 2004). However, this blend did not attract any males in field trapping experiments in Taiwan (Schläger et al. 2012), Thailand, or Vietnam (Srinivasan et al. 2015). These findings suggest geographic variation in the pheromone blend between Asian and Beninese *M. vitrata* populations. Geographic variation has been reported recently in two different Chinese populations: females from Wuhan produced a pheromone ratio of 100:12.1:79.5 *EE*10,12-16:Ald : *EE*10,12-16:OH : *E*10-16:Ald, whereas a ratio of 100:0.7:10.3 was found in gland extracts from females from Huazhou (Lu et al. 2013).

Since the ratio of the pheromone components is crucial to design efficient lures (Baker 2008), the aim of this study was to determine whether there is geographic variation in the sexual communication of *M. vitrata*, specifically between Asian (Taiwan, Thailand, and Vietnam) and West African (Benin) populations. Single female pheromone gland extracts were analyzed by gas chromatography–mass spectrometry (GC/MS), and pheromone components were identified and quantified by comparison to all authentic stereoisomers of the three described pheromone compounds for *M. vitrata*. Male preference was assessed by performing wind tunnel experiments to compare responses of males from Taiwan and Benin to females and gland extracts from the two populations.

5.3 Methods and Materials

Insects

Larvae and pupae of *M. vitrata* were obtained from laboratory colonies at AVRDC - The World Vegetable Center in Taiwan and Thailand; the Vietnam Academy of Agricultural Sciences in Ha Noi, Vietnam; and the International Institute of Tropical Agriculture in Cotonou, Benin. At the Leibniz Institute of Vegetable and Ornamental Crops in Großbeeren (IGZ), Germany, the larvae were reared individually in small plastic cups (37 ml, Market Grounds GmbH & Co. KG, Hamburg, Germany) for at least one generation on artificial cowpea diet until pupation. The diet was prepared as described in Jackai and Raulston (1988), with three modifications. We added saccharose to the diet, but did not add dried and pulverized cowpea leaves, and used kanamycin (Sigma-Aldrich Chemie GmbH, Taufkirchen, Germany) as antibiotic. The pupae were transferred to acrylic glass or glass cages where the emerging moths mated. For oviposition, females were placed singly in small plastic cups (37 ml). For experiments, pupae were placed separately in plastic cups (37 ml) directly after pupation and reared under a 14L:10D photoperiod at 25 °C and 80 % relative humidity in a controlled environment chamber (Vötsch, Balingen, Germany). After emergence, moths were kept under the same conditions, and were provided with a 10 % honey solution from a cotton dental roll (Apodiscounter, Markkleeberg, Germany) as food.

Pheromone Gland Extraction

Pheromone glands were excised from 4- to 5-d-old, unmated female moths 5–6 h into scotophase. Behavioral observations confirmed calling behavior of females from Benin and Taiwan during this time. Glands were transferred singly to a 150 µl conical glass insert (Macherey-Nagel GmbH & Co. KG, Düren, Germany) containing 50 µl hexane (≥98.0 %, Merck KGaA, Darmstadt, Germany) with 1 ng pentadecane (Sigma-Aldrich Chemie GmbH, Taufkirchen, Germany) as internal standard. Glands were extracted for 30–40 min at room temperature in 1.5 ml brown glass vials (Macherey-Nagel GmbH & Co. KG, Düren, Germany) to prevent photoisomerization of conjugated diene systems (Cork et al. 1988; Ideses and Shani 1988; Cork 2004). Samples were analyzed immediately by gas chromatography coupled with mass spectrometry (GC/MS) or were stored at −80 °C for up to 2 d until analysis.

Reference Compounds

The synthetic standards *EE-* (isomeric purity: 98 %), ZZ10,12-16:Ald (95 %), *EE-* (98 %), and ZZ10,12-16:OH (93 %) were purchased from Pherobank, Wageningen, Netherlands. *EZ-* (97 %), ZE10,12-16:Ald (97 %), *EZ-* (87 %), ZE10,12-16:OH (92 %), *Z-* (78 %), and *E*10-16:Ald (96 %) were obtained from the Biocontrol Research Laboratories, Bangalore, India. The isomeric purity was determined by GC/MS analysis. All synthetic compounds were verified using NMR spectroscopy at the Max Planck Institute for Chemical Ecology (MPICE).

Chemical Analysis of Female Gland Extracts

Single gland extracts were analyzed by GC/MS using selected ion monitoring (SIM) to increase sensitivity. This method is suitable to detect trace compounds, such as minor pheromone compounds. A glass syringe (10 µl, Hamilton, Höchst, Germany) was rinsed × 10 with acetone (≥99.8 %, Merck KGaA, Darmstadt, Germany) and × 10 with hexane (≥98.0 %, Merck KGaA, Darmstadt, Germany), after which 1 µl octane (Sigma-Aldrich Chemie GmbH, Taufkirchen, Germany) was taken up into the syringe. The gland extract was reduced under a gentle stream of nitrogen to 2–4 µl, and transferred with the syringe to a 150 µl glass insert (Macherey-Nagel GmbH & Co. KG, Düren, Germany) in a 1.5 ml brown crimp-capped vial (Macherey-Nagel GmbH & Co. KG, Düren, Germany). Samples were analyzed using an Agilent 7890A gas chromatograph equipped with a Supelcowax column (60 m×0.25 mm ID, 0.25 µm film thickness, Sigma-Aldrich Chemie GmbH, Taufkirchen, Germany) and coupled with an Agilent 5975C mass selective detector (MSD). The carrier gas was helium at a constant flow of 1.2 ml/min. Samples were analyzed by injecting the entire volume (i.e., 3–5 µl) in splitless mode at 250 °C inlet temperature. The oven program was optimized for separation of all standard compounds: 70 °C held for 1 min, increased at 5 °C/min to 240 °C and held for 10 min to clean the column. SIM was conducted focusing on unique or most abundant ions of the internal standard and the pheromone components: pentadecane (m/z 57, 212), hexadecenal (m/z 55, 69, 238), hexadecadienal, (m/z 67, 81, 236), and hexadecadienol (m/z 67, 81, 238). Each ion was monitored individually at the expected retention times of the compounds and their isomers. Retention times were determined by injecting multicomponent standard mixtures containing 0.1, 0.5, 1, 2.5, 5, and 7.5 ng of each component together with 1 ng of the internal standard. The quantity of each compound in single gland extracts was determined by relating its peak area to the internal standard and correcting for the differential responsiveness of the MSD to the compound. Pheromone quantities below the detection limit

(<0.01 ng) were scored as zero, and such samples were excluded from statistical analysis. Additionally, one combined and concentrated gland extract of 19 *M. vitrata* females from Taiwan was analyzed under the same conditions.

Male Attraction in Wind Tunnel Assays

Cross-attraction between Asian and West African *M. vitrata* populations was determined with the populations from Benin and Taiwan only. Wind tunnel assays were conducted by using both live female moths and their gland extracts as source of pheromone. The custom-made wind tunnel (80 cm long × 35.5 cm high × 37.5 cm wide) was made of glass, except for one long side which was made of polypropylene with two closable windows to be able to exchange the moths and gland extracts (mechanical workshop, MPICE). An airflow of ~0.03 m/s was generated by an axial fan (REW 150/2, axial in-duct fan 150 mm, 6 in 1 PH, Helios, Villingen-Schwenningen, Germany) in the wind tunnel. Incoming air was cleaned using active charcoal (double filter for range hoods, Ewald Wolf Kunststoffwerk GmbH & CO. KG, Weißenburg in Bayern, Germany). A strip of light-emitting diodes (λ=625 nm, Barthelme GmbH & Co, Nürnberg, Germany) was placed on top of the tunnel to provide illumination. Experiments were conducted in an environment–controlled climate chamber (Johnson Controls International, Essen, Germany) at 25 °C and 80 % relative humidity. Every experimental day before scotophase, the wind tunnel was cleaned with 70 % ethanol ($\geq$99.8 % with 1 % methyl ethyl ketone, Carl Roth GMBH+ CO. KG, Karlsruhe, Germany) while air was flowing through the tunnel.

Females and males were placed in the chamber for at least 1.5 h prior to the experiment. Containers with confined females were covered by a layer of active charcoal (double filter for range hoods, Ewald Wolf Kunststoffwerk GmbH & CO. KG, Weißenburg in Bayern, Germany) to prevent contaminations of pheromone components inside the climate chamber. Bioassays were performed between 5 and 10 h into the scotophase. Four- to 6-d-old males were released individually from small plastic cups (37 ml) 52 cm downwind from the pheromone source. If a male did not take flight within 10 min, he was scored as a non-responder. After taking flight, moth behavior was observed for up to 10 min. Males from Benin and Taiwan were tested alternately and each individual was tested only once. The male response was divided into the following behavioral categories: (1) taking flight but not orienting toward the source of stimuli; (2) oriented flight, ending in hovering in front of the pheromone source; and (3) pheromone source contact.

No-choice Assay with Live Females

Four- to 6-d-old females were caged singly inside a translucent, horizontally placed plastic cup (473 ml) near the upwind end of the tunnel in the middle of the cross section. The bottom of the plastic cup and the lid consisted of gauze to enable airflow through the plastic cup. The female was observed continuously during the experiment for showing calling behavior (extruding her ovipositor) and was replaced if she did not call.

No-choice Assay with Gland Extracts

Gland extracts prepared as described above from 4- to 5-d-old virgin females also were used as a pheromone source. These gland extracts were used in the experiment within 24 h to make sure that the pheromone compounds would not have degraded. Gland extracts, which were not used on the same day, were stored in sealed, brown vials (Macherey-Nagel GmbH & Co. KG, Düren, Germany) at −80 °C. Up to 10 glands from females belonging to the same population were extracted together in hexane for 30 to 40 min. Gland extracts of 2 to 29 females were merged and adjusted to a concentration of one gland equivalent in 5 µl, which was applied on a 1 cm^2 triangle of filter paper (VWR International GmbH, Dresden, Germany). This paper was suspended from a wire at the upwind end of the tunnel. Filter paper with 5 µl pure hexane served as a control.

Two-choice Bioassay

Females from Benin and Taiwan or the corresponding gland extracts prepared as described above were offered simultaneously in the wind tunnel to males from both populations. The distance between the plastic cups with females in the wind tunnel was 1 cm; filter papers with gland extracts were placed 10 cm apart. Experiments were conducted as described above.

Statistical Analysis

Statistical analysis was conducted using SAS 9.4. Pheromone quantities and pheromone ratios were log(x+0.01) transformed and analyzed using the nonparametric Kruskal-Wallis test with Bonferroni correction for pairwise multiple comparisons because data were not always normally distributed. To analyze behavioral data, the number of male moths recorded for each behavioral category in the wind tunnel was subjected to a two-tailed 2×2 Fisher's exact test.

5.4 Results

Chemical Analysis of Pheromone Gland Extracts

GC/MS analyses revealed that *EE*10,12-16:Ald and *EE*10,12-16:OH were present in gland extracts of all four *M. vitrata* populations (Fig. 1). *EE*10,12-16:Ald was the major pheromone component accounting for 91.4 % (for Benin) to 92.4 % (for Thailand) of the pheromone blend. The minor component *EE*10,12-16:OH was always present in gland extracts of females from Benin, but could not be detected in 19 % (7) of the Vietnam samples, in 9 % (7) of the Thailand samples, or in 2 % (1) of the Taiwan samples. *E*10-16:Ald, previously described as a pheromone component, was not detected in any sample. Analysis of a pooled and concentrated gland extract of 19 females from Taiwan confirmed that the amount of this compound was below the detection level (data not shown). Amounts of the stereoisomers of the three pheromone components also were below the detection limit.

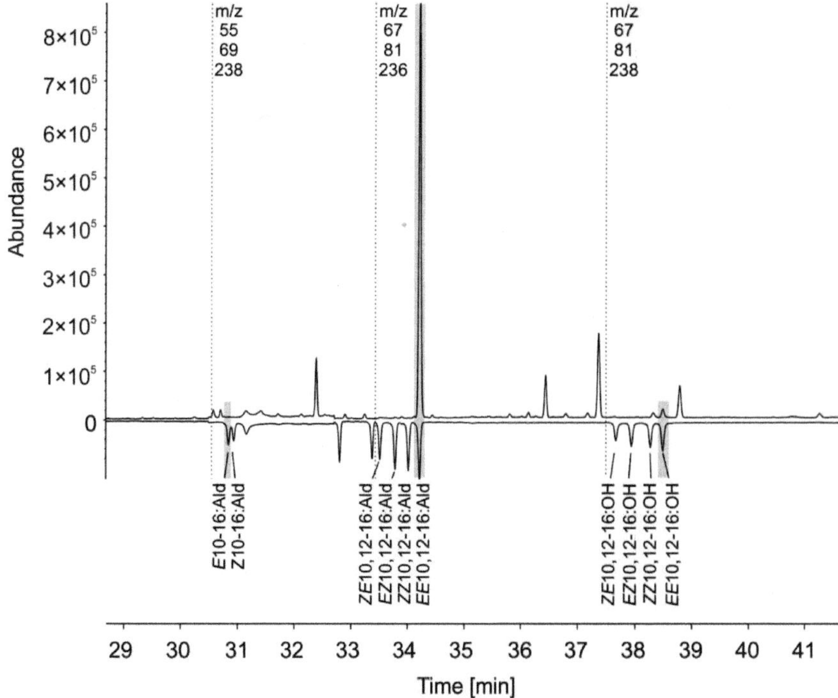

Figure 1 GC/MS selected ion chromatograms of a single gland extract of *Maruca vitrata* (Benin; top) and the multicomponent standard mixture (1 ng/µl; inverted). *Dotted lines* indicate monitoring of a new group of selected ions. Peaks highlighted by a grey color correspond to compounds reported to be sex pheromone components for *M. vitrata*.

The total amount of pheromone detected per gland differed significantly between the populations ($P \leq 0.001$). Females from Benin (N=60) and Taiwan (N=59) produced significantly more pheromone compared to females from Thailand (N=71) and Vietnam (N=30), and females from Vietnam produced the least (Fig. 2a). The ratio of *EE*10,12-16:Ald to *EE*10,12-16:OH also differed among populations (Kruskal-Wallis test, P=0.04). However, pairwise multiple comparisons with Bonferroni correction showed no difference between specific populations (P=0.39 - 1) (Fig. 2b).

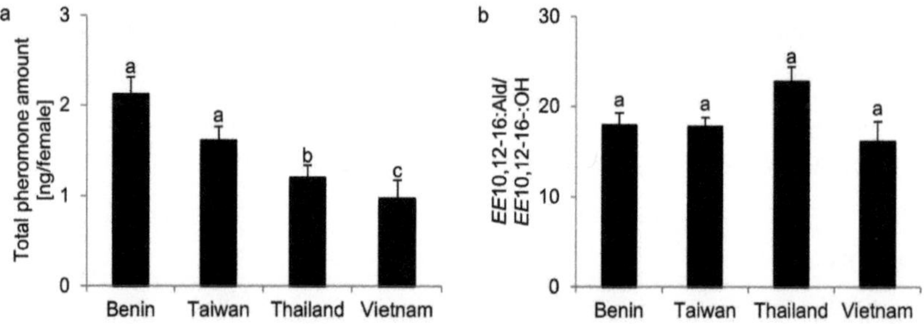

Figure 2 Comparisons (mean±SE) of the pheromone amount (a) and ratio (b) of *Maruca vitrata* females from populations of Benin (N=60), Taiwan (N=59), Thailand (N=71), and Vietnam (N=30). Bars with the same letter are not significantly different according to Kruskal-Wallis test followed by Bonferroni correction ($P \leq 0.05$).

Behavioral Experiments with Live Females

In no-choice experiments, males from Benin (N=48) (Fig. 3a) and Taiwan (N=52) (Fig. 3b) responded similarly to calling females from both regions, although significantly more males from Benin took flight in tests with females from Taiwan (Fig. 3a). In two-choice assays, males from Benin (N=41) did not discriminate between females from Taiwan or Benin (Fig. 3c), while *M. vitrata* males from Taiwan (N=63) hovered significantly more often in front of their own females. There was no difference regarding the frequencies of source contact (Fig. 3d, Table S1).

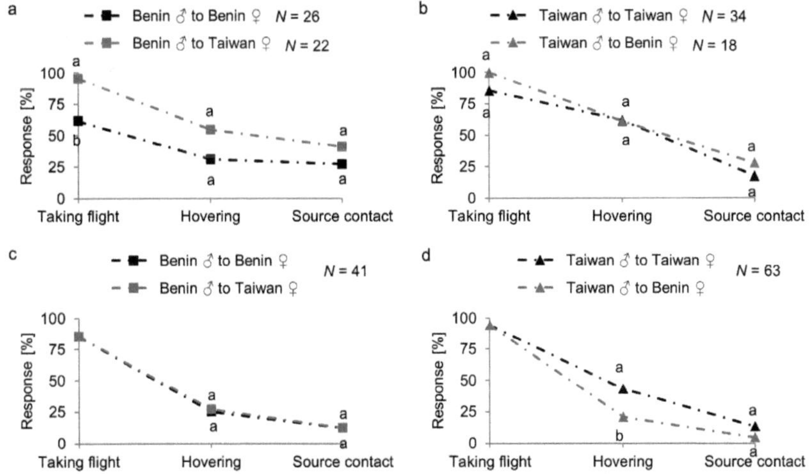

Figure 3 Behavioral responses of *Maruca vitrata* males from Benin (no-choice: **a** two-choice assay: **c**) and Taiwan (no-choice: **b** two-choice assay: **d**) towards calling females from Benin or/and Taiwan given as percentages. Symbols in the same behavioral category with different letters were significantly different according to Fisher's exact test, two tailed ($P \leq 0.05$).

Behavioral Experiments with Gland Extracts

In control experiments with pure solvent, no hovering or source contact was observed (data not shown). In no-choice assays, males from Benin responded equally to gland extracts from both regions ($N=81$) (Fig. 4a). This time, males from Taiwan ($N=80$) hovered significantly more often in front of gland extracts of females from Benin compared to gland extracts from Taiwan, but they contacted both sources equally often (Fig. 4b, Table S2). In two-choice assays, both males from Benin ($N=36$) and Taiwan ($N=35$) did not discriminate between gland extracts from both regions (Fig. 4c, d).

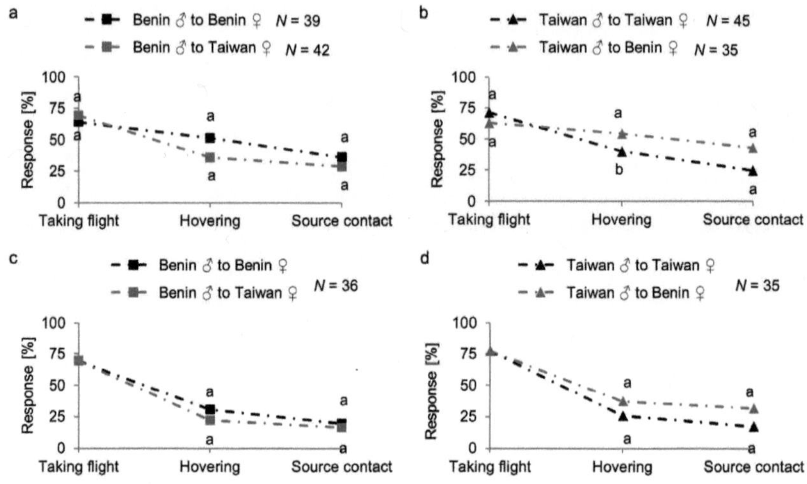

Figure 4 Behavioral responses of *Maruca vitrata* males from Benin (no-choice: **a** two-choice assay: **c**) and Taiwan (no-choice: **b** two-choice assay: **d**) towards pheromone gland extracts from females from Benin or/and Taiwan applied on filter paper. Symbols in the same behavioral category with different letters were significantly different according to Fisher's exact test, two-tailed ($P \leq 0.05$).

5.5 Discussion

In previous work on the sex pheromone of female *M. vitrata*, up to three compounds, *EE*10,12-16:Ald, *EE*10,12-16:OH and *E*10-16:Ald have been reported as potential pheromone components. Downham et al. (2003) first reported *E*10-16:Ald but only could detect it in GC/EAD and EAG analyses of pheromone gland extract from females from a mixed population from Benin, Nigeria, India, and Taiwan, and could not detect it in GC/MS analyses. Downham et al. (2003, 2004) found that a blend of the three components in a ratio of 100:5:5, respectively, was the most attractive synthetic lure in wind tunnel assays and field trapping experiments in Benin. We only detected *EE*10,12-16:Ald and *EE*10,12-16:OH in our GC/MS analyses of pheromone gland extracts and *E*10-16:Ald was not detected (<0.01 ng) in any of our samples. Similarly, Adati and Tatsuki (1999) did not detect *E*10-16:Ald in gland extracts of female *M. vitrata* from Ghana, but, recently, Lu et al. (2013) detected *E*10-16:Ald in single female gland extracts from two Chinese *M. vitrata* populations by GC/MS. The aldehyde constituted 10.3 % of the pheromone gland extract of females from Huazhou, while in females from Wuhan *E*10-16:Ald was the major component at 79.5 %. In field studies in China, the number of males caught also was highest when *E*10-16:Ald was added: in Huazhou, a 100:10:10-blend (*EE*10,12-16:Ald : *EE*10,12-16:OH : *E*10-16:Ald) attracted the maximum number of males, whereas in Wuhan a 100:10:80-blend was most attractive (Lu et al. 2013).

In our study, the ratio of both detected pheromone components, *EE*10,12-16:Ald to *EE*10,12-16:OH, did not vary among the investigated *M. vitrata* populations. *EE*10,12-16:OH was a minor compound and ranged from 10.1 % in females from Thailand to 11.5 % in females from Taiwan, compared to *EE*10,12-16:Ald (100 %). Pheromone ratios are known to be affected by the time of gland extraction in the scotophase as well as the age of the female (Delisle and Royer 1994; Kamimura and Tatsuki 1993), thus making it difficult to compare different studies. However, variations in the extraction times could at least partly explain differences in relative amounts of the pheromone components. A combined gland extract of *M. vitrata* females from Ghana contained 3–4 % of *EE*10,12-16:OH (Adati and Tatsuki 1999). The shorter extraction time of the pheromone glands (10 min) compared to our extraction time (30–40 min) possibly led to a lower amount of the alcohol. *EE*10,12-16:OH is more polar than *EE*10,12-16:Ald and might need more time to dissolve in the nonpolar solvent hexane. Downham et al. (2003) also found a lower percent of the alcohol (2–5 %) in a pooled gland extract of the mixed *M. vitrata* population, where they used a shorter extraction time (5–10 min), albeit with a brief sonication during the solvent extraction. Lu et al. (2013) extracted single pheromone glands of Chinese *M. vitrata* females for a longer time period (30 min) and found a similar percentage of *EE*10,12-16:OH (12.1 %) in females from Wuhan. Females from Huazhou contained the lowest proportion of the alcohol (0.7 %) detected in a *M. vitrata* population so far.

We did not perform pheromone collection by air entrainment because of the low pheromone amounts detected in individual glands (0.03–6.3 ng/female). Downham et al. (2003) collected volatiles by air entrainment from 1 to 2 calling *M. vitrata* females on activated charcoal (5 mg; 0.01 mm particle size) or from 12 to 22 females on Porapak Q (50–80 mesh; 100 mg). These authors detected only *EE*10,12-16:Ald, although in much lower amounts compared to the merged gland extract (0.5–2 ng/female). However, subsequent experiments revealed that only 44 % of synthetic *EE*10,12–16:Ald were recovered from activated charcoal filters, but over 90 % from Porapak Q filters (Downham et al. 2003).

In our behavioral assays, *M. vitrata* males from Taiwan and Benin responded similarly to females from both regions and to the corresponding gland extracts. The behavioral response of male *M. vitrata* to live females and gland extracts was comparable, which verifies our extraction method for the chemical pheromone blend analysis. Visual cues also may affect male response, as males were hovering longer in front of calling females compared to gland extracts applied on filter paper. Together, our results do not support the hypothesis of geographic variation in the sexual communication between Asian and West African *M. vitrata* populations. However, this conclusion is drawn with caution, because in artificial wind tunnel experiments *Agrotis ipsilon* (Hufnagel) males also were equally attracted to geographically distinct females with significantly different pheromone blends (Gemeno et al. 2000), while recent field experiments in China did show geographic variation in attraction of *A. ipsilon* males (Du et al. 2015).

It is possible that additional, unidentified pheromone components are essential for the attraction of *M. vitrata* males, because reported trap catches of *M. vitrata* males generally are very low. For example, in a period of eight weeks the 100:5:5-blend attracted only a total of 33.1 males per trap in Benin (Downham et al. 2003). In China, only 19.5 males in total per trap were caught in four weeks (Lu et al. 2013). In contrast, we caught up to 89 males in traps baited with live females in one night (unpublished results). However, traps baited with the

100:5:5-blend attracted significantly more *M. vitrata* males than traps baited with two virgin females in field trapping experiments in Benin (Downham et al. 2003). The authors assumed that females were not constantly releasing pheromones compared to the synthetic lure. In our experiments, only females caged in large plastic cups (250 ml) attracted males, while females confined in smaller cages (96 or 37 ml) did not attract any males. A similar effect might be responsible for the low attractiveness of live females used as baits in field experiments in Benin.

Another possible explanation for the low trap catches with synthetic pheromone blends is the presence of isomeric impurities that may inhibit male attraction. *EE*10,12-16:Ald and *EE*10,12-16:OH contain conjugated diene systems that are susceptible to photoisomerization induced by sunlight (Cork 2004). Pheromone lures for field studies in Benin (Downham et al. 2003), China (Lu et al. 2013), Taiwan (Schläger et al. 2012), Thailand, and Vietnam (Srinivasan et al. 2015) were not formulated with UV-stabilizers to prevent photoisomerization. Adati and Tatsuki (1999) reported that *M. vitrata* males were more attracted to purified *EE*10,12-16:Ald (isomeric purity 99 %) than to unpurified *EE*10,12-16:Ald (92 %) in behavioral bioassays. Furthermore, the presence of stereoisomers reduced male attraction, especially when adding *EZ*10,12-16:Ald to *EE*10,12-16:Ald (Adati and Tatsuki 1999). In field bioassays with *Earias vittella* (F.), the addition of an isomer (*EZ*10,12-16:Ald) to the major pheromone component *EE*10,12:16Ald also significantly reduced trap catches (Cork et al. 1988). However, trap catches of *M. vitrata* males in field studies in Benin were not affected by different isomeric purities of *EE*10,12-16:Ald and *EE*10,12-16:OH (73 %, 80 %, 91 %, or >99 %) (Downham et al. 2004). Additionally, pheromone lures for field trapping experiments in Benin were wrapped in aluminium foil to prevent photoisomerization (Downham et al. 2003, 2004), but again there was no difference between male trap catches with protected or exposed pheromone dispensers (Downham et al. 2004).

In summary, our studies revealed no significant differences in the relative amounts of the three compounds previously reported as components of the female sex pheromone in extracts of pheromone glands of female *M. vitrata* from colonies originating in Taiwan, Thailand, Vietnam, or Benin. Furthermore, in our behavioral assays, *M. vitrata* males from Taiwan and Benin responded similarly to females from both regions and to the corresponding gland extracts. Hence, we do not support the hypothesis that there is geographic variation in sex pheromone blends among *M. vitrata* populations from Asia and West Africa although a recent study indicated the presence of different putative subspecies in *M. vitrata* in Asia and sub-Saharan Africa based on mitochondrial cytochrome oxidase I (COI) gene sequences (Periasamy et al. 2015). Future research should focus on the possibility of additional pheromone components that are essential to attract males, and on the verification of pheromone purity and stability under field conditions.

5.6 Supplementary Material

Table S1 Behavioral responses of Taiwanese or Beninese *M. vitrata* males to live females from both regions

Set up	Origin of the male	N	Behavioral category	P
No-choice	Benin	48	Taking flight	**0.0063**
			Hovering	0.7463
			Source contact	0.6186
	Taiwan	52	Taking flight	0.1504
			Hovering	0.5243
			Source contact	0.4424
Two choice assay	Benin	41	Hovering	1
			Source contact	1
	Taiwan	63	Hovering	**0.0081**
			Source contact	0.7199

Bold data indicate significant differences in behavioral responses of males between females from Taiwan and Benin (Fishers exact test, two-tailed, $P \leq 0.05$)

Table S2 Behavioral responses of Taiwanese or Beninese *M. vitrata* males to female gland extracts from both regions

Set up	Origin of the male	N	Behavioral category	P
No-choice	Benin	81	Taking flight	0.6465
			Hovering	0.0799
			Source contact	0.7003
	Taiwan	80	Taking flight	0.4773
			Hovering	**0.0352**
			Source contact	0.2953
Two choice assay	Benin	36	Hovering	0.5607
			Source contact	1
	Taiwan	35	Hovering	0.4064
			Source contact	0.609

Bold data indicate significant differences in behavioral responses of males between gland extracts of females from Taiwan and Benin (Fishers exact test, two-tailed, $P \leq 0.05$).

6 Chapter VI
General Discussion

Objective of this thesis was the improvement of pheromone traps for monitoring *Maruca vitrata* in tropical Asia, where synthetic lures failed to attract males so far. Within the scope of this work, possible geographic variation in the sexual communication system between *M. vitrata* populations from West Africa and Asia was investigated. In this chapter, the major findings are discussed in a broader context and targets for future research are suggested.

<u>Improvement of Pheromone Traps for Monitoring *Maruca vitrata* in Tropical Asia</u>

Pheromone-based pest monitoring is an important component of integrated pest management, *i.e.* control measures are not performed until the pest species causes an economic damage on the crop plant (economic threshold level) (Boller et al. 2004). The species-specificity of pheromone lures is a great advantage, enabling highly selective pest monitoring. In general, a reliable monitoring system needs standardized parameters regarding the attractant, trap height, trap type and trap location (Cork 2004).

So far, trap catches of *M. vitrata* using synthetic pheromone lures were very low (Downham et al. 2003; Lu et al. 2013), or traps did not attract any males at all (Schläger et al. 2012; Srinivasan et al. 2015). Previous work focused on the sex pheromone of West African *M. vitrata* populations. Here, I investigated predominantly the sexual communication system of a Taiwanese *M. vitrata* population as a representative for the Asian region. Synthetic lures failed to attract *M. vitrata* males in Taiwan and several other Asian countries (Schläger et al. 2012; Srinivasan et al. 2015); however, delta traps baited with virgin females and placed at a height of 180 cm caught high numbers of males in yard long bean (*Vigna unguiculata* spp. *sesquipedalis*) fields in Taiwan (Chapter 2). This result shows that delta traps have the appropriate design for trapping *M. vitrata*.

The optimal release device ensures storage and a moderate release of the pheromone components under field conditions (Cork 2004). Furthermore, the release device protects the pheromone compounds from degradation and/or isomerization by embedding in the matrix or, more frequently, pheromone blends are merged with antioxidants and/or UV light-stabilizers (Jones 1998; Cork 2004). The present work shows that a synthetic blend of the three described *M. vitrata* pheromone components was stable on rubber septa and polyethylene vials under storage conditions (6 weeks) and under simulated field conditions (1 week) when merged with the antioxidant butylated hydroxytoluene (Chapter 4). The observed isomerization of EE10,12-16:Ald and EE10,12-16:OH was minimal under both conditions. Long term studies are now necessary to investigate the chemical stability and release rate of pheromone compounds from dispensers to evaluate lure longevity and determine replacement time in the field.

Considering the fact that synthetic pheromone lures attracted only very few or no *M. vitrata* males in the field, it is possible that the pheromone blend required for short- and/or long-range attraction has not been fully identified so far. For example, the pheromone ratio as detected by gland extractions may not reflect the pheromone blend released by the female. Headspace collections of calling females by closed-loop stripping could reveal the pheromone blends to which males respond in the field (Löfstedt 1990). However, pheromone collection by air entrainment reported in previous studies revealed that much lower amounts were obtained from *M. vitrata* females compared to gland extractions (Downham et al. 2003). Unknown active pheromone components may be another reason for the low attractiveness of synthetic pheromone lures. The analysis of electrophysiological responses from *M. vitrata* male antennae to female gland extracts by gas chromatography – electroantennographic detection (GC–EAD) may be a powerful tool to detect putative new pheromone compounds. However, in own GC–EAD experiments, I was not able to establish antennal responses from males using synthetic pheromone compounds (e.g. *EE*10,12-16:Ald) (data not shown) which elicited clear responses in dose-response tests by EAG recordings (Chapter 2). Also in previous studies, results of GC–EAD experiments performed with *M. vitrata* to identify pheromone compounds were not clear (Downham et al. 2003) or were not shown (Adati and Tatsuki 1999). On the other hand, antennae of *M. vitrata* females and males responded clearly to different host plant volatiles in GC–EAD experiments (Wang et al. 2014; Bendera et al. 2015). In order to successfully utilize GC–EAD to determine the presence of additional pheromone compounds in gland extracts in the future, the current method requires optimization. Alternatively, pheromones sampled by solvent extraction or headspace collection could be fractionated using a preparative fraction collector coupled to a GC. The obtained fractions are then monitored for active compounds by EAG measurements. EAG-active fractions are subsequently analyzed by mass spectrometry to identify the active compounds.

In several moth species, the addition of host plant volatiles to synthetic lures was shown to increase male attraction in the field (Dickens et al. 1993; Light et al. 1993). Whether this is also the case for *M. vitrata* males is not known. In tropical Asia, *M. vitrata* is a major pest on yard long beans (Schreinemachers et al. 2014). For evaluation of attractants composed of pheromone components and plant semiochemicals, attraction of *M. vitrata* males towards emitted volatiles of yard long beans should to be investigated.

Host plant volatiles can also stimulate female pheromone production and release (Landolt and Phillips 1997; Reddy and Guerrero 2004). These effects have not been investigated in *M. vitrata* females so far. However, a recent study with a *M. vitrata* population from Kenya and their local host plant cowpea showed that the presence of cowpea seedlings, cowpea leaf extracts, as well as the cowpea leaf volatile 1-octen-3-ol alone increased mating (Bendera et al. 2015). In our field experiments, males were clearly attracted to traps baited only with virgin females (Chapter 2) which contradict the need of host plant volatiles to achieve male attraction. The possible role of plant semiochemicals in sexual attraction of *M. vitrata* males needs to be investigated in future experiments.

Geographic Variation in the Sexual Communication System between Asian and West African *Maruca vitrata* Populations

Sex pheromone blends may vary among populations of the same moth species (McElfresh and Millar 1999; Gemeno et al. 2000; El-Sayed et al. 2003; Cortés et al. 2010). Two types of pheromone blend variation can be distinguished: Monomorphic variation, which occurs more frequently, is caused by shifted ratios of the same pheromone components, whereas polymorphic variation defines pheromone blends with structurally distinct pheromone components (Löfstedt 1990).

Previous findings suggest that pheromone blends vary between *M. vitrata* populations from West Africa and Asia. In field trapping experiments in Benin, *M. vitrata* males were attracted to a synthetic pheromone blend of *EE*10,12-16:Ald, *EE*10,12-16:OH, and *E*10-16:Ald in a ratio 100:5:5 (Downham et al. 2003), while this blend did not attract any *M. vitrata* males in Taiwan (Schläger et al. 2012), Thailand and Vietnam (Srinivasan et al. 2015). A comparative study of two geographically different Chinese *M. vitrata* populations indeed recently revealed geographic variation in the pheromone blends (Lu et al. 2013). Females from Huazhou produced a pheromone ratio of 100:0.7:10.3, whereas the pheromone ratio of females from Wuhan comprised a high proportion of *E*10-16:Ald: 100:12.1:79.5. The different pheromone blends were confirmed in subsequent field studies. A 100:10:10-blend attracted the highest number of males from Huazhou, whereas males from Wuhan were mainly attracted by the 100:10:80-blend. *E*10-16:Ald was only detected in both Chinese *M. vitrata* populations by GC–MS (Lu et al. 2013). Evidences for its role as a pheromone component in West African insect populations are based on EAG measurements, behavioral bioassays, and field studies (Adati and Tatsuki 1999; Downham et al. 2003 and 2004).

Although in a first phylogenetic analysis of mitochondrial cytochrome oxidase I (COI) sequences, *M. vitrata* populations from West Africa (Niger, Nigeria, and Burkina Faso) and Taiwan formed a single clade (Margam et al. 2010), a recent study revealed genetic differences between West African and Asian populations based on COI (Periasamy et al. 2015) as well as the protein arrestin-2 (Chang and Srinivasan 2013). Genetic differences between geographically different populations of the same species may also indicate differences regarding the pheromone communication, but the pheromone composition detected in females from Benin, Taiwan, Thailand, and Vietnam did not differ significantly (Chapter 5). Surprisingly, the minor compound *E*10-16:Ald (Downham et al. 2003 and 2004; Lu et al. 2013) was not detected in any gland extract. Either the sensitivity of the GC–MS method was not sufficient to detect very low quantities of *E*10-16:Ald (detection limit: < 0.01 ng), or this compound is not produced by *M. vitrata* females from the four target countries.

It is possible, that additional, not yet identified compounds are responsible for pheromone blend variation between *M. vitrata* populations from Asia and West Africa. Apart from *E*10-16:Ald; (*E*)-11-hexadecenal, and (*Z*)- as well as (*E*)-12-hexadecenal elicited high responses from male antennae of a mixed *M. vitrata* population in EAG measurements (Downham et al. 2003). Hence, re-investigations of monounsaturated hexadecenals as putative pheromone components may be relevant. Further approaches to detect additional pheromone components have been discussed in the previous section.

In wind tunnel assays, I found that *M. vitrata* males from Taiwan and Benin were attracted towards live females as well as female gland extracts from both regions. These findings are in agreement with the similar pheromone ratio of females from Taiwan and Benin. The attractiveness of the identified pheromone blend of *EE*10,12-16:Ald: *EE*10,12-16:OH in a ratio of 100:10 should be evaluated for males from Benin and Taiwan in future wind tunnel experiments. In general, the short-range attraction to lures is monitored in wind tunnel assays, whereas field studies also include long-range attraction. Taiwanese males may respond to a distinct pheromone ratio and/or additional, not yet detected pheromone components.

In conclusion, the results of this thesis do not support the presence of geographic variation in the sexual communication between Asian and West African *M. vitrata* populations. However, future research should focus on the elucidation of key factors which are essential for sexual attraction of *M. vitrata* males in the field, particularly with regard to the optimization of pheromone lures for pest monitoring in both regions.

7 References

Adati T and Tatsuki S (1999) Identification of female sex pheromone of the legume pod borer, *Maruca vitrata* and antagonistic effects of geometrical isomers. Journal of Chemical Ecology 25: 105–116

Adati T, Nakamura S, Tamò M and Kawazu K (2004) Effect of temperature on development and survival of the legume pod borer, *Maruca vitrata* (Fabricius) (Lepidoptera: Pyralidae) reared on a semi-synthetic diet. Applied Entomology and Zoology 39 (1): 139-145

Adekola OF and Oluleye F (2008) Induced tolerance of cowpea mutants to *Maruca vitrata* (Fabricius) (Lepidoptera : Pyralidae). African Journal of Biotechnology 7 (7): 878-883

Afun JVK, Jackai LEN and Hodgson CJ (1991) Calendar and monitored insecticide application for the control of cowpea pests. Crop Protection 10: 363-370

Ando T, Inomata S-i and Yamamoto M (2004) Lepidopteran sex pheromones. In: Schulz S (ed) Chemistry of pheromones and other semiochemicals I. Berlin; Heidelberg: Springer-Verlag: 51-96

Ando T and Yamakawa R (2011) Analyses of lepidopteran sex pheromones by mass spectrometry. Trends in Analytical Chemistry 30 (7): 992-1002

Asiwe JAN, Nokoe S, Jackai LEN and Ewete FK (2005) Does varying cowpea spacing provide better protection against cowpea pests? Crop Protection 24 (5): 465-471

Baker TC (2008) Balanced olfactory antagonism as a concept for understanding evolutionary shifts in moth sex pheromone blends. Journal of Chemical Ecology 34 (7): 971-981

Bendera M, Ekesi S, Ndung'u M, Srinivasan R and Torto B (2015) A major host plant volatile, 1-octen-3-ol, contributes to mating in the legume pod borer, *Maruca vitrata* (Fabricius) (Lepidoptera: Crambidae). The Science of Nature 102 (9-10): 1-10

Boller EF, Avilla J, Joerg E, Malavolta C, Wijnands FG and Esbjerg P (2004) Integrated production: principles and technical guidelines IOBC/wprs Bulletin Vol. 27 (2): 31-49

Bottenberg H, Tamò M and Singh BB (1998) Occurrence of phytophagous insects on wild *Vigna* sp. and cultivated cowpea: comparing the relative importance of host-plant resistance and millet intercropping. Agriculture Ecosystems & Environment 70 (2-3): 217-229

Chang JC and Ramasamy S (2013) Molecular-phylogenetic characterization of arrestin-2 from *Maruca vitrata* (Lepidoptera: Crambidae). Annals of the Entomological Society of America 106 (3): 359-370

Cork A (2004) Pheromone manual. Natural Resources Institute, Chatham Maritime ME4 4TB, UK

Cork A, Alam SN, Das A, Das CS, Ghosh GC, Farman DI, Hall DR, Maslen NR, Vedham K, Phythian SJ, Rouf FMA and Srinivasan K (2001) Female sex pheromone of brinjal fruit and shoot borer, *Leucinodes orbonalis* blend optimization. Journal of Chemical Ecology 27 (9): 1867-1877

Cork A, Chamberlain DJ, Beevor PS, Hall DR, Nesbitt BF, Campion DG and Attique MR (1988) Components of female sex pheromone of spotted bollworm, *Earias vittella* F. (Lepidoptera: Noctuidae): Identification and field evaluation in Pakistan. Journal of Chemical Ecology 14 (3): 929-945

Cortés Palacio AM, Zarbin PHG, Takiya DM, Bento JMS, Guidolin AS and Consoli FL (2010) Geographic variation of sex pheromone and mitochondrial DNA in *Diatraea saccharalis* (Fab., 1794) (Lepidoptera: Crambidae). Journal of Insect Physiology 56 (11): 1624-1630

Dannon EA, Tamò M, van Huis A and Dicke M (2010 a) Functional response and life history parameters of *Apanteles taragamae*, a larval parasitoid of *Maruca vitrata*. Biocontrol 55: 363-378

Dannon EA, Tamò M, van Huis A and Dicke M (2010 b) Effects of volatiles from *Maruca vitrata* larvae and caterpillar-infested flowers of their host plant *Vigna unguiculata* on the foraging behavior of the parasitoid *Apanteles taragamae*. Journal of Chemical Ecology 36: 1083-1091

Dannon EA, Tamò M, van Huis A and Dicke M (2012 a) Assessing non-target effects and host feeding of the exotic parasitoid *Apanteles taragamae*, a potential biological control agent of the cowpea pod borer *Maruca vitrata*. Biocontrol 57: 415-425

Dannon EA, Tamò M, Agboton C, van Huis A and Dicke M (2012 b) Effect of *Maruca vitrata* (Lepidoptera: Crambidae) host plants on life-history parameters of the parasitoid *Apanteles taragamae* (Hymenoptera: Braconidae). Insect Science 19 (4): 518-528

Delisle J and Royer L (1994) Changes in pheromone titer of obliquebanded leafroller, *Choristoneura rosaceana,* virgin females as a function of time of day, age, and temperature. Journal of Chemical Ecology 20 (1): 45-69

Dickens JC, Smith JW and Light DM (1993) Green leaf volatiles enhance sex attractant pheromone of the tobacco budworm, *Heliothis virescens* (Lepidoptera: Noctuidae) Chemoecology 4: 175-177

Downham MCA, Hall DR, Chamberlain DJ, Cork A, Farman DI, Tamò M, Dahounto D, Datinon B and Adetonah S (2003) Minor components in the sex pheromone of legume pod-borer: *Maruca vitrata* development of an attractive blend. Journal of Chemical Ecology 29: 989–1012

Downham MCA, Tamò M, Hall DR, Datinon B, Adetonah S and Farman DI (2004) Developing pheromone traps and lures for *Maruca vitrata* in Benin, West Africa. Entomologia Experimentalis et Applicata 110: 151-158

Du Y, Feng B, Li H, Liu C, Zeng J, Pan L and Yu Q (2015) Field evaluation of *Agrotis ipsilon* (Lepidoptera: Noctuidae) pheromone blends and their application to monitoring moth populations in China. Environmental Entomology 44 (3): 724-733

Ekesi S (1999) Insecticide resistance in field populations of the legume pod-borer, *Maruca vitrata* Fabricius (Lepidoptera: Pyralidae), on cowpea, *Vigna unguiculata* (L.), Walp in Nigeria. International Journal of Pest Management 45 (1): 57-59

Ekesi S (2000) Effect of volatiles and crude extracts of different plant materials on egg viability of *Maruca vitrata* and *Clavigralla tomentosicollis*. Phytoparasitica 28 (4): 305-310

Ekesi S, Adamu RS and Maniania NK (2002) Ovicidal activity of entomopathogenic hyphomycetes to the legume pod borer, *Maruca vitrata* and the pod sucking bug, *Clavigralla tomentosicollis*. Crop Protection 21 (7): 589-595

El-Sayed AM, Delisle J, De Lury N, Gut LJ, Judd GJR, Legrand S, Reissig WH, Roelofs WL, Unelius CR and Trimble RM (2003) Geographic variation in pheromone chemistry, antennal electrophysiology, and pheromone-mediated trap catch of North American populations of the obliquebanded leafroller. Environmental Entomology 32 (3): 470-476

Fery FL (2002) New opportunities in *Vigna*. In: Janick J and Whipkey A (eds) Trends in new crops and new uses. ASHS Press, Alexandria, VA. pp. 424–428

Fujita K and Ofosu-Budu KG (1996) Significance of legumes in intercropping systems. In: Ito O, Johansen C, Adu-Gyamfi JJ, Katayama K, Kumar Rao JVDK and Rego TJ (eds). Dynamics of roots and nitrogen in cropping systems of the semi-arid tropics. Japan International Research Center for Agricultural Sciences. International Agriculture Series No. 3. pp 20-40

Gemeno C, Lutfallah AF and Haynes KF (2000) Pheromone blend variation and cross-attraction among populations of the black cutworm moth (Lepidoptera: Noctuidae). Annals of the Entomological Society of America 93 (6): 1322-1328

Giller KE (2001) Nitrogen fixation in tropical cropping systems. CAB International, Wallingford, UK

Groot AT (2014) Circadian rhythms of sexual activities in moths: a review. Frontiers in Ecology and Evolution 2 (43)

Hajek A (2004) Natural enemies – An introduction to biological control. Cambridge University Press

Hartwig NL and Ammon HU (2002) Cover crops and living mulches. Weed Science 50 (6): 688-699

Himeno K and Honda H (1992) (*E,Z*)-10,12-Hexadecadienals and (*E,E*)-10,12-Hexadecadienals, major components of female sex pheromone of the cotton leaf-roller, *Notarcha derogata* (Fabricius) (Lepidoptera, Pyralidae). Applied Entomology and Zoology 27 (4): 507-515

Howse PE (1998) Pheromones and behaviour. In: Howse PE, Stevens IDR and Jones OT (eds) Insect pheromones and their use in pest management. Chapmann and Hall

Huang CC, Peng WK and Talekar NS (2003) Parasitoids and other natural enemies of *Maruca vitrata* feeding on *Sesbania cannabina* in Taiwan. Biocontrol 48 (4): 407-416

Ideses R and Shani A (1988) Chemical protection of pheromones containing an internal conjugated diene system from isomerization and oxidation. Journal of Chemical Ecology 14 (8): 1657-1669

Jackai LEN and Raulston JR (1988) Rearing the legume pod borer *Maruca testulalis* (Geyer) (Lepidoptera: Pyralidae) on artificial diet. Agricultural Research 34: 168-172

Jackai LEN, Ochieng RS and Raulston JR (1990) Mating and oviposition behaviour in the legume pod borer, *Maruca testulalis*. Entomologia Experimentalis et Applicata 56: 179-186

Jackai LEN, Padulosi S and Ng Q (1996) Resistance to the legume pod borer, *Maruca vitrata* Fabricius, and the probable modalities involved in wild *Vigna*. Crop Protection 15 (8): 753-761

Jones OT (1998) Practical applications of pheromones and other semiochemicals. In: Howse PE, Stevens IDR, and Jones OT (eds) Insect pheromones and their use in pest management. Chapmann and Hall

Jurenka R (2004) Insect pheromone biosynthesis. In: Schulz S (ed) Chemistry of pheromones and other semiochemicals I. Berlin; Heidelberg: Springer-Verlag

Kaissling KE (1971) Insect Olfaction. In: L. M Beidler (ed.) Handbook of sensory physiology Vol. IV. Chemical senses. Springer Verlag, Berlin. pp 351-431

Kamimura M and Tatsuki S (1993) Diel rhythms of calling behavior and pheromone production of oriental tobacco budworm moth, *Helicoverpa assulta* (Lepidoptera: Noctuidae). Journal of Chemical Ecology 19 (12): 2953-2962

Karel AK (1993) Effects of intercropping with maize on the incidence and damage caused by pod borers of common beans. Environmental Entomology 22 (5): 1076-1083

Karlson P and Lüscher M (1959) 'Pheromones': a New Term for a Class of Biologically Active Substances. Nature 183: 55-56

Kawazu K, Otuka A, Adati T, Tonogouchi H and Yase J (2008) Lepidoptera captured on the East China Sea in 2005 and predicted migration sources. Entomological Science 11: 315–322

Landolt PJ and Phillips TW (1997) Host plant influences on sex pheromone behavior of phytophagous insects. Annual Review of Entomology (42): 371-391

Leal WS (2005) Pheromone reception. In: Schulz S (ed) Chemistry of pheromones and other semiochemicals II. Berlin; Heidelberg: Springer-Verlag. pp 1-36

Lee ST, Srinivasan R, Wu YJ and Talekar NS (2007) Occurrence and characterization of a nucleopolyhedrovirus from *Maruca vitrata* (Lepidoptera, Pyralidae) isolated in Taiwan. Biocontrol 52 (6): 801-819

Light DM, Flath RA, Buttery RG, Zalom FG, Rice RE, Dickens JC and Jang EB (1993) Host-plant green-leaf volatiles synergize the synthetic sex pheromones of the corn earworm and codling moth (Lepidoptera). Chemoecology 4: 145-152

Löfstedt C (1990) Population variation and genetic control of pheromone communication systems in moths. Entomologia Experimentalis et Applicata 54 (3): 199-218

Lu P-F, Qiao H-L, Wang X-P, Wang X-Q and Lei C-L (2007) The emergence and mating rhythms of the legume pod borer, *Maruca vitrata* (Fabricius, 1787) (Lepidoptera: Pyralidae). The Pan-Pacific Entomologist 83 (3): 226–234

Lu P-F, Qiao H-L and Lei C-L (2008) Daily rhythms of mating and of the stimulatory activity of the female pheromone release on male antennae in the legume pod borer, *Maruca vitrata* (Lepidoptera : Pyralidae). Entomologia Generalis 31 (1): 49-62

Lu P-F, Qiao H-L and Luo Y-Q (2013) Female sex pheromone blends and male response of the legume pod borer *Maruca vitrata* (Lepidoptera: Crambidae), in two populations of mainland China. Zeitschrift für Naturforschung C 68: 416-427

Margam VM, Coates BS, Ba MN, Sun W, Binso-Dabire CL, Baoua I, Ishiyaku MF, Shukle JT, Hellmich RL, Covas FG, Srinivasan R, Armstrong J, Pittendrigh BR and Murdock LL (2010) Geographic distribution of phylogenetically-distinct legume pod borer, *Maruca vitrata* (Lepidoptera: Pyraloidea: Crambidae). Molecular Biology Reports 38 (2): 893-903

McElfresh JS and Millar J (1999) Geographic variation in sex pheromone blend of *Hemileuca electra* from Southern California. Journal of Chemical Ecology 25 (11): 2505-2525

Mehinto JT, Atachi P, Kpindou OKD and Tamò M (2014) Pathogenicity of entomopathogenic fungi *Metarhizium anisopliae* and *Beauveria bassiana* on larvae of the legume pod borer *Maruca vitrata* (Lepidoptera: Crambidae). Asian Research Publishing Network. Journal of Agricultural and Biological Science 9 (2): 55-64

Murlis J, Elkinton JS and Cardé RT (1992) Odor plumes and how insects use them. Annual Review of Entomology 37 (1): 505-532

Periasamy M, Schafleitner R, Krishnan M and Srinivasan R (2015) Phylogeographical structure in mitochondrial DNA of legume pod borer (*Maruca vitrata*) population in tropical Asia and sub-Saharan Africa. PLoS ONE 10 (4):e0124057

Rafaeli A and Jurenka RA (2003) PBAN regulation of pheromone biosynthesis in female moths. In: Blomquist GJ and Vogt RG (eds) Insect pheromone biochemistry and molecular biology: The biosynthesis and detection of pheromones and plant volatiles. London: Elsevier Academic Press: 107-136

Rafaeli A (2005) Mechanisms involved in the control of pheromone production in female moths: recent developments. Entomologia Experimentalis et Applicata 115 (1): 7-15

Raina AK, Wergin WP, Murphy CA and Erbe EF (2000) Structural organization of the sex pheromone gland in *Helicoverpa zea* in relation to pheromone production and release. Arthropod Structure & Development 29 (4): 343-353

Rauscher S and Arn H (2001) Reproducibility and shelf-life of pheromone lures. Pheromones for Insect Control in Orchards and Vineyards. In: Withgall P (ed) IOBC WPRS Bulletin Vol. 24(2):1-4. Pheromones and other biological techniques for insect control in orchards and vineyards. Working group "Use of pheromones and other semiochemicals in integrated control", Proceedings of the meeting in Hohenheim (Baden-Württemberg, Germany), 10-12 November, 1999

Reddy GVP and Guerrero A (2004) Interactions of insect pheromones and plant semiochemicals. Trends in Plant Science 9 (5): 253-261

Schläger S, Ulrichs C, Srinivasan R, Beran F, Bhanu KRM, Mewis I and Schreiner M (2012) Developing pheromone traps and lures for *Maruca vitrata* in Taiwan. Gesunde Pflanze 64 (4): 183-186

Sharma HC (1998) Bionomics, host plant resistance, and management of the legume pod borer, *Maruca vitrata* — a review. Crop Protection 17 (5): 373-386

Sharma HC, Saxena KB and Bhagwat VR (1999) The legume pod borer, *Maruca vitrata*: bionomics and management. Information Bulletin no. 55 (In En. Summaries in En, Fr.). Patancheru 502 324, Andhra Pradesh, India: International Crops Research Institute for the Semi-Arid Tropics. ISBN 92-9066-406-1. Order code IBE 055

Schreinemachers P, Srinivasan R, Wu M-H, Bhattarai M, Patricio R, Yule S, Quang VH and Hop BTH (2014) Safe and sustainable management of legume pests and diseases in Thailand and Vietnam: a situational analysis. International Journal of Tropical Insect Science 34 (2): 88–97

Srinivasan R (2008) Susceptibility of legume pod borer (LPB), *Maruca vitrata* to delta-endotoxins of Bacillus thuringiensis (Bt) in Taiwan. Journal Invertebrate Pathology 97: 79-81

Srinivasan R, Yule S, Chang JC, Periasamy M, Lin MY, Hsu YS, Schafleitner R (2013) Towards developing a sustainable management strategy for legume pod borer, *Maruca vitrata* on yard-long bean in Southeast Asia. In: Holmer R, Linwattana G, Nath P, Keatinge JDH (eds) Proceedings of the Regional Symposium on High Value Vegetables in Southeast Asia: Production, Supply and Demand (SEAVEG2012), 24–26 January 2012, Chiang Mai, Thailand. AVRDC—The World Vegetable Center, Publication No. 12–758. AVRDC – The World Vegetable Center, Taiwan. pp 76–82

Srinivasan R, Lin M-Y, Su F-C, Yule S, Khumsuwan C, Hien T, Hai VM, Khanh LD and Bhanu KRM (2015) Use of insect pheromones in vegetable pest management: Successes and struggles. In: Chakravarthy AK (ed) New horizons in insect science: Towards sustainable pest management. Springer India. pp. 231-237

Stevens IDR (1998) Chemical aspects of pheromones. In: Howse PE, Stevens IDR, and Jones OT (eds) Insect pheromones and their use in pest management. Chapmann and Hall

Sumberg J (2002) The logic of fodder legumes in Africa. Food Policy 27: 285-300

Tumuhaise V, Ekesi S, Mohamed SA, Ndegwa PN, Irungu LW, Srinivasan R and Maniania NK (2015) Pathogenicity and performance of two candidate isolates of *Metarhizium anisopliae* and *Beauveria bassiana* (Hypocreales: Clavicipitaceae) in four liquid culture media for the management of the legume pod borer *Maruca vitrata* (Lepidoptera: Crambidae). International Journal of Tropical Insect Science 35 (1): 34-47

Ulrichs C, Mewis I, Schnitzler WH and Burleigh JR (2001) Effectivity of synthetic insecticides against *Maruca vitrata* F. and the parasitoid *Bassus asper* CHOU & SHARKEY in the Philippines. Mitteilungen der Deutschen Gesellschaft für Allgemeine und Angewandte Entomologie 13: 1-6

Vrkoč J, Konečný K, Valterová I and Hrdý I (1988) Rubber substrates and their influence on isomerization of conjugated dienes in pheromone dispensers. Journal of Chemical Ecology 14 (5): 1347-1358

Wang P, Zhang N, Zhou L-L, Si S-Y, Lei C-L, Ai H and Wang X-P (2014) Antennal and behavioral responses of female *Maruca vitrata* to the floral volatiles of *Vigna unguiculata* and *Lablab purpureus*. Entomologia Experimentalis et Applicata 152 (3): 248-257

Wills RBH, Wong AWK, Scriven FM and Greenfield H (1984) Nutrient composition of Chinese vegetables. Journal of Agricultural and Food Chemistry 32 (2): 413-416

Winch T (2007) Growing Food – A guide to food production. Springer. p 150

Witzgall P (2001) Pheromones - future techniques for insect control? Pheromones for insect control in orchards and vineyards. IOBC WPRS Bulletin Vol. 24(2): 114-122

Yule S and Srinivasan R (2013) Evaluation of bio-pesticides against legume pod borer, *Maruca vitrata* Fabricius (Lepidoptera: Pyralidae), in laboratory and field conditions in Thailand. Journal of Asia-Pacific Entomology 16 (4): 357-360

8 Summary

The legume pod borer, *Maruca vitrata* F. (Lepidoptera: Crambidae), cause severe damage on economically important legume crops in the tropics. This pest species is mainly controlled by synthetic insecticides but without satisfying results. Monitoring by pheromone traps can help to perform target-oriented control measures. (E,E)-10,12-hexadecadienal, (E,E)-10,12-hexadecadienol and (E)-10-hexadecenal have been described as pheromone components. A blend of these compounds in a ratio 100:5:5 was the most attractive lure in field studies in Benin, whereas synthetic lures failed to attract *M. vitrata* males in tropical Asia so far. For developing an efficient pheromone lure in this region, a Taiwanese *M. vitrata* population was investigated as a representative for the Asian region. Taiwanese males responded to all described pheromone compounds in electroantennographic measurements. However, the 100:5:5-blend and the major pheromone component (E,E)-10,12-hexadecadienal alone did not attract males in field trapping experiments in Taiwan. In contrast, high numbers of males were caught in delta traps baited with live virgin females. A chemical analysis of female gland extracts confirmed the presence of the three pheromone components in *M. vitrata* populations from Taiwan and Thailand by gas chromatography – flame ionization detection, but the ratios differed from the one attracting males in Benin. However, the corresponding synthetic lures did not attract *M. vitrata* males in subsequent field bioassays in Taiwan. A stability test of the pheromone blend loaded together with butylated hydroxytoluene as antioxidant on rubber septa or polyethylene vials revealed that the three pheromone compounds did not degrade under storage conditions in six weeks and under simulated field conditions in one week. Due to the fact that the 100:5:5-blend attracted males in field studies Benin, but not in Taiwan, Thailand, and Vietnam, a possible geographic variation in the pheromone blend between Asian and West African *M. vitrata* populations was investigated. Therefore, pheromone gland extracts of females from Taiwan, Thailand, Vietnam, and Benin were analyzed by gas chromatography – mass spectrometry. The chemical analysis revealed only the presence of (E,E)-10,12-hexadecadienal and (E,E)-10,12-hexadecadienol. The ratio of both detected components did not vary among the four target populations. Moreover, responses of males from Taiwan and Benin were compared to calling females and gland extracts of females from both regions in wind tunnel assays. Taiwanese and Beninese males were similarly attracted to all pheromone sources. In summary, the study did not support geographic variation in the sexual communication between West African and Asian *M. vitrata* populations.

9 Zusammenfassung

Der Leguminosenbohrer, *Maruca vitrata* F. (Lepidoptera: Crambidae), richtet schwerwiegende Frassschäden an wirtschaftlich bedeutenden Hülsenfrüchtlern in den Tropen an. Die Schädlingskontrolle erfolgt hauptsächlich durch den Einsatz synthetischer Insektizide, jedoch ohne befriedigendes Ergebnis. Ein Monitoring mit Pheromonfallen kann dabei helfen Kontrollmaßnahmen zielgerichtet durchzuführen. (*E,E*)-10,12-Hexadecadienal, (*E,E*)-10,12-Hexadecadienol und (*E*)-10-Hexadecenal wurden als Komponenten des Sexualpheromons von *M. vitrata* beschrieben. Ein synthetischer Lockstoff bestehend aus diesen Verbindungen in einem Verhältnis von 100:5:5 erzielte die höchsten Fallenfänge in einer Feldstudie in Benin in Westafrika. Im tropischen Asien hingegen konnten bisher keine *M. vitrata* Männchen mit Hilfe synthetischer Pheromonlockstoffe gefangen werden. Im Rahmen dieser Arbeit wurde das Sexualpheromon verschiedener asiatischer *M. vitrata* Populationen untersucht mit dem Ziel einen effektiven Lockstoff für diese Regionen zu entwickeln. Elektrophysiologische Untersuchungen zeigten, dass die Antennen von *M. vitrata* Männchen einer taiwanesischen Population alle drei beschriebenen Pheromonkomponenten detektieren können. Die stärkste elektrophysiologische Antwort der Antenne wurde durch (*E,E*)-10,12-Hexadecadienal ausgelöst. In Feldversuchen in Taiwan waren allerdings weder die 100:5:5-Mischung, noch (*E,E*)-10,12-Hexadecadienal allein attraktiv. Jedoch wurden hohe Fänge mit Deltafallen erzielt, die mit jungfräulichen *M. vitrata* Weibchen bestückt waren. In einer chemischen Analyse der weiblichen Drüsenextrakte konnten die drei Pheromonkomponenten in *M. vitrata* Populationen aus Taiwan und Thailand durch Gaschromatographie – Flammenionizationsdetektion gefunden werden. Das Verhältnis der Komponenten unterschied sich aber von dem, welches die Männchen in Benin angelockt hatte. Die entsprechenden synthetischen Lockstoffe erzielten keine Fallenfänge in Feldstudien in Taiwan. Da die synthetischen Pheromonkomponenten insbesondere unter Feldbedingungen instabil sein könnten, wurde ein Stabilitätstest durchgeführt. Dazu wurden die Pheromonkomponenten zusammen mit dem Antioxidans Butylhydroxytoluol auf Gummisepten oder Polyethylenröhrchen aufgetragen. Die Ergebnisse zeigten, dass sie unter Lagerungsbedingungen über sechs Wochen und unter simulierten Feldbedingungen über eine Woche stabil waren. Da die 100:5:5-Mischung der Pheromonkomponenten in Feldstudien in Benin attraktiv war, nicht aber in Taiwan, Thailand, und Vietnam, wurde vermutet, dass sich die Zusammensetzung des Sexualpheromons zwischen den asiatischen und westafrikanischen *M. vitrata* Populationen unterscheidet. Um dies zu untersuchen, wurden Drüsenextrakte von *M. vitrata* Weibchen aus Taiwan, Thailand, Vietnam, und Benin mittels Gaschromatographie

– Massenspektrometrie analysiert und verglichen. Bei diesen Untersuchungen konnten nur (*E,E*)-10,12-Hexadecadienal und (*E,E*)-10,12-Hexadecadienol in den Drüsenextrakten nachgewiesen werden. Das Verhältnis beider Komponenten unterschied sich nicht signifikant zwischen den vier Insektenpopulationen. In Windtunnelexperimenten wurde außerdem gezeigt, dass sich Männchen aus Taiwan und Benin ähnlich gegenüber paarungsbereiten Weibchen oder deren Drüsenextrakten beider Populationen verhalten. Zusammenfassend lässt sich festhalten, dass die Untersuchung einen geographischen Unterschied in der sexuellen Kommunikation zwischen asiatischen und westafrikanischen *M. vitrata* Populationen nicht unterstützen kann.

10 Acknowledgments

Mit der Fertigstellung der Dissertation ist es Zeit nochmal denjenigen zu danken, die mich begleitet und unterstützt haben.

Zuerst will ich meinem Doktorvater Prof. Dr. Dr. Christian Ulrichs und meiner Betreuerin Dr. Inga Mewis danken, dass sie mir die Möglichkeit gegeben haben an dieser spannenden Thematik zu arbeiten und für die stete Unterstützung in meinem Promotionsvorhaben.

Dr. Stefan Kühne vom Julius Kühn-Institut für Strategien und Folgenabschätzung danke ich für die Übernahme des Zweitgutachtens.

Ein großer Dank geht an Prof. Dr. Monika Schreiner vom Leibniz Institut für Gemüse- und Zierpflanzenbau in Großbeeren/Erfurt e.V. (IGZ) für die Möglichkeiten der räumlichen und technischen Nutzung am IGZ, sowie für die Unterstützung bei der Finanzierung.

Ich danke meinen Kollegen aus der Abteilung Qualität für die Hilfsbereitschaft und die nette Arbeitsatmosphäre. Insbesondere danke ich Annett Platalla für die Einführung in die GC-MS und die Hilfe im Labor und Andrea Maikath für die Hilfe bei den Insektenzuchten. Des Weiteren danke ich Holger Brand und Jörg Bigus für die Einrichtung des Insektariums und Sieglinde Widiger, Ingo Hauschild und Thomas Runge für die Hilfe bei der Nutzung der Klimaschränke und -kammern.

Für die Unterstützung bei den Insektenzuchten danke ich meinen HiWis, Nick Arndt, Cindy Auricht und insbesondere Vanessa Hörmann, die auch bei der Vorbereitung der ersten Feldversuche in Taiwan eine große Hilfe war.

Ein besonderer Dank geht an Dr. Franziska Beran von der Abteilung Entomologie am Max Planck Institut für chemische Ökologie (MPICE) für die Einführung in die GC-EAD und EAG, die wertvollen Ratschläge, die Korrekturen der Arbeiten und die konstante Unterstützung.

Special thanks belong to Dr. Astrid T. Groot from the Entomology Department at MPICE for the introduction in the pheromone blend analysis in her lab. Moreover, I am grateful for her valuable advices, interesting discussions, and the enthusiasm.

Ich danke Daniel Veit von der Werkstatt des MPICE für den Bau des Windtunnels und die Ratschläge. Bei Dr. Christian Paetz aus der Forschungsgruppe Biosynthese/NMR des MPICE will ich mich für die spektroskopische Untersuchung der synthetischen Pheromon-Verbindungen bedanken.

I am grateful to Prof. Dr. Bill Hansson from the Department of Evolutionary Neuroethology at MPICE for giving me the opportunity to perform GC-EAD and EAG in his lab.

I am very grateful for the help and support during my stay at AVRDC-The World Vegetable Center in Taiwan from Dr. Ramasamy Srinivasan, Lin Mei-ying, Yang Li-hua, Su Fu-cheng, and all the staff of the Entomology Unit.

For the supply of test insects, I would like to thank Dr. Manuele Tamò and Benjamin Datinon from International Institute of Tropical Agriculture in Cotonou, Dr. Sopana Yule from AVRDC-The World Vegetable Center in Bangkok, Dr. Vu Manh Hai and Dr. Le Duc Khanh from the Vietnam Academy of Agricultural Sciences in Ha Noi, and Dr. Mohamad Roff Mohd. Noor from the Malaysian Agricultural Research and Development Institute in Kuala Lumpur.

I wish to thank Dr. Bhanu R. M. Karumuru from the Biocontrol Research Laboratories in Bangalore for providing the synthetic pheromone compounds and the pheromone lures for the first field studies in Taiwan.

Für die finanzielle Unterstützung des Projektes danke ich der Deutschen Gesellschaft für Internationale Zusammenarbeit und dem Leibniz-Institut für Gemüse- und Zierpflanzenbau Großbeeren/Erfurt e.V.. Ich danke dem Deutschen Akademischen Austauschdienst für die gewährten Kurzzeitstipendien und der FAZIT-Stiftung für das gewährte Abschlussstipendium.

Meinen Freunden danke ich fürs Zuhören und die moralische Unterstützung.

Abschließend will ich meinen Eltern und meinen Schwestern Nadin und Sabrina für das Verständnis und die Motivation danken.

11 Selbstständigkeitserklärung

Die vorliegende Arbeit wurde von mir selbst, und nur unter Verwendung der angegebenen Quellen und Hilfsmittel erstellt.

Diese Arbeit wurde nicht zuvor bei einer anderen Hochschule als Dissertation eingereicht.

Die geltende Promotionsordnung (Nr.24/2005) der Lebenswissenschaftlichen Fakultät der Humboldt-Universität zu Berlin ist mir bekannt.

Ich erkläre weiterhin, dass ich noch keinen Doktorgrad erlangt oder zu erlangen versucht habe.

Berlin, den 28.09.2015

Stefanie Schläger

In der Reihe *Berliner ökophysiologische und phytomedizinische Schriften* sind bisher erschienen:

Band 01:   Mohammad Mahir Uddin (2009)
Chemical ecology of mustard leaf beetle Phaedon cochleariae (F.).
ISBN 978-3-89959-848-3.

Band 02:   Ilir Morina (2009)
Entwicklung von Verfahren zur Rekultivierung der Aschedeponie des Braunkohlekraftwerks in Prishtina (Kosovo).
ISBN 978-3-89959-872-8.

Band 03:   Melanie Wiesner (2009)
Veränderungen gesundheitsrelevanter Inhaltsstoffe in *Parthenium hysterophorus* L. in Abhängigkeit von der Pflanzengröße und Klimafaktoren.
ISBN 978-3-89959-880-3.

Band 04:   Fransika Rohr (2009)
Variabilität aliphatischer Glucosinolate in *Arabidopsis thaliana*-Ökotypen und deren Einfluss auf die Wirtspflanzeneignung von zwei folivoren Insektenarten.
ISBN 978-3-89959-884-9.

Band 05:   Jutta Buchhop (2009)
Characterization of phylogenetically diverse CLRV-isolates by RFLP and research into identification of two isometric viruses.
ISBN 978-3-89959-929-9.

Band 06:   Nora Koim (2010)
Urban sprawl, land cover change and forest fragmentation – Case study Pereira, Colombia.
ISBN 978-3-89959-955-8.

Band 07:   Nadja Förster (2010)
Eignung unterschiedlicher salicylathaltiger *Salix*-Klone für die Arzneimittelindustrie.
ISBN 978-3-89959-964-0.

Band 08:   Jana Gentkow (2010)
Cherry leaf roll virus (CLRV): Charakterisierung ausgewählter Virusisolate unter besonderer Berücksichtigung des viralen Hüllproteins.
ISBN 978-3-89959-976-3.

Band 09:   Ahmad Fakhro (2010)
Interaction of Pepino mosaic virus (PepMV) and fungal root endophytes with tomato hosts (*Lycopersicum esculentum* Mill.).
ISBN 978-3-89959-995-4.

Band 10:   Stefan Irrgang (2010)
Mikro- und makroskopische Untersuchungen an Veredelungsstellen von Straßenbäumen im Hinblick auf die Beeinflussung ihrer Bruchsicherheit.
ISBN 978-3-89959-998-5.

Band 11:   Julia Jahnke (2010)
Guerilla Gardening anhand von Beispielen in New York, London und Berlin.
ISBN 978-3-86247-001-3.

Band 12:   Astrid Karoline Günther (2010)
            Analysen zur Intensität der Pflanzenschutzmittel-Anwendung und Aufklärung
            ihrer Einflussfaktoren in ausgewählten Ackerbaubetrieben.
            ISBN 978-3-86247-005-1.

Band 13:   Milena A. Dimova (2010)
            Untersuchungen zur Epidemiologie von *Pythium aphanidermatum* in
            Abhängigkeit von den Umgebungsbedingungen bei der Gewächshausgurke
            (*Cucumis sativus* L.).
            ISBN 978-3-86247-033-4.

Band 14:   Claudia Patricia Pérez-Rodríguez (2010)
            Physiologische Veränderungen in Früchten der Solanaceaengewächse in
            Abhängigkeit von physikalischen Elicitoren während der Produktion und nach
            der Ernte.
            ISBN 978-3-86247-066-2.

Band 15:   Charles Adarkwah (2010)
            Integrated management of the stored-product pest insects *Corcyra cephalonica*,
            Cadra cautella, *Sitophilus zeamais* and *Tribolium castaneum* by use of the
            parasitic wasps *Habrobracon hebetor*, *Venturia canescens*, *Lariophagus
            distinguendus* and neem seed oil.
            ISBN 978-3-86247-077-8.

Band 16:   Christoph von Studzinski (2010)
            Angewandte Methoden der xenovegetativen Vermehrung.
            ISBN 978-3-86247-088-4.

Band 17:   Tanja Mucha-Pelzer (2011)
            Amorphe Silikate – Möglichkeiten des Einsatzes im Gartenbau zur
            physikalischen Schädlingsbekämpfung.
            ISBN 978- 3-86247-106-5.

Band 18:   Diego Miranda (2011)
            Effect of salt stress on physiological parameters of cape gooseberry, *Physalis
            peruviana* L.
            ISBN 978- 3-86247-119-5

Band 19:   Franziska Beran (2011)
            Host preference and aggregation behavior of the striped flea beetle, *Phyllotreta
            striolata*.
            ISBN 978- 3-86247-188-1

Band 20:   Mohammed Abul Monjur Khan (2011)
            Induced biochemical changes and gene expression in *Brassica oleracea* and
            Arabidopsis thaliana by drought stress and its consequences on resistance to
            aphids.
            ISBN 978- 3-86247-203-1.

Band 21:   Sandra Lerche (2012)
            Untersuchungen zur Anwendung, Praxiseinführung und molekularen
            Identifizierung von Stamm V24 des entomopathogenen Pilzes *Lecanicillium
            muscarium* (Petch) Zare & W. Gams.
            ISBN 978- 3-86247-248-2.

Band 22:   Carsten Richter (2012)
            Entwicklung und Überprüfung eines gasdichten Küvettensystems für
            Experimente unter hochgradig kontrollierten Bedingungen mit
            Gaswechselmessungen.
            ISBN 978- 3-86247-271-0.

Band 23:   Aksana Grineva (2012)
            Influence of the two stored grain pest insects *Sitophilus granarius* and
            Oryzaephilus surinamensis on temperature, relative humidity, moisture
            content, and mould growth in stored triticale.
            ISBN 978- 3-86247-279-6.

Band 24:   Carmen Büttner & Christian Ulrichs (2012)
            Aktuelle Themen in Landwirtschaft und Gartenbau am Beispiel von Südtirol.
            ISBN 978- 3-86247-279-6.

Band 25:   Juliane Langer (2012)
            Molecular and epidemiological characterisation of Cherry leaf roll virus
            (CLRV).
            ISBN 978- 3-86247-279-6.

Band 26:   Franziska Rohr-Doucet (2012)
            AOP-Variabilität in *Arabidopsis thaliana*-Kreuzungslinien – Auswirkungen
            auf die Resistenz gegenüber verschieden spezialisierten Lepidopteren-Arten.
            ISBN 978- 3-86247-329-8.

Band 27:   Vanessa Hörmann (2012)
            Lignin als biologische Barriere gegen Schimmelpize in Innenräumen.
            ISBN 978- 3-86247-330-4.

Band 28:   Jacqueline Kurth (2013)
            Auswirkungen verschiedener Düngerzusammensetzungen auf den Ertrag bei
            Schnittrosen unter Berücksichtigung des Anbauverfahrens.
            ISBN 978- 3-86247-336-6.

Band 29:   Juliane Langer, Carmen Büttner & Christian Ulrichs (2014)
            Kolumbien – klimatische und politische Voraussetzungen für eine
            landwirtschaftliche Produktion.
            ISBN 978- 3-86247-430-1.

Band 30:   Heike Luisa Dieckmann (2014)
            Detection of the European mountain ash ringspot associated virus (EMARaV)
            in Sorbus aucuparia L. in several European contries.
            ISBN 978- 3-86247-441-7.

Band 31:   Rima Marion Baag (2014)
            Analyse von trans-Resveratrol in historischen Rebsorten der Weinanbaugebiete
            Sachsen und Saale-Unstrut.
            ISBN 978- 3-86247-488-2.

Band 32:   Ayesha Rahmann (2014)
            Study of the protective effects of nano-structured silica and plant derived
            biomolecules on nuclear polyhedrosis virus affected silkworm larvae at the
            behavioral and molecular level.
            ISBN 978- 3-86247-495-0.

Band 33:   Bettina Gramberg (2015)
               Weiterentwicklung eines elektrochemischen Biosensors zum Nachweis von
               Pflanzenviren und Insektiziden.
               ISBN 978- 3-86247-512-4.

Band 34:   Wilhelm van Husen (2015)
               Artspezifische Aufnahme und Verteilung von Cadmium bei indigenen
               afrikanischen Gemüsearten und daraus abzuleitende Ernährungsempfehlungen.
               ISBN 978- 3-86247-523-0.

Band 35:   Jenny Roßbach (2015)
               European mountain ash ringspot-associated viras (EMARaV): diversity and
               geographic distribution in Europe.
               ISBN 978- 3-86247-547-6.

Band 36:   Silke Steinmöller (2015)
               Risikominderung der Verbreitung von Quarantäneschadorganismen der
               Kartoffel durch hygienisierende Maßnahmen.
               ISBN 978- 3-86247-550-6.

Band 37:   Christin Siewert (2016)
               Genomic and functional analysis of species within the Acholeplasmataceae –
               Phytoplasmas and Acholeplasmas.
               ISBN 978- 3-86247-579-7.

Band 38:   Angela Köhler (2016)
               Untersuchungen zur Phenolglycosidkonzentration ausgewählter intra- und
               interspezifischer Kreuzungen salicinreicher Biomasseweiden.
               ISBN 978- 3-86247-581-0.

Band 39:   Nicolas Meyer (2016)
               Vergleichende ökophysiologische Untersuchung verschiedener Baumarten zur
               Verwendung als Straßenbegleitgrün in Berlin.
               ISBN 978- 3-86247-586-5.